Inside
INFORMATION

Worship Wars, Calvinism, Elder Rule and much more!

By

John R. Bisagno

CONTENTS

CHAPTER

Chapter 1

It's Tearing Us Apart

At age 14, I joined the First Baptist Church of Perry, Oklahoma. I was baptized, became fairly active, but did not actually become a Christian until four years later. My most distinct memory is the controversy that went on all through high school about dancing and going to movies. Little did I imagine that controversy and division would continue to be the predominant image of my beloved denomination these 55 years later.

When I was called to preach, I began commuting from Tulsa, Oklahoma, where I was a traveling evangelist, to Midwestern Seminary in Kansas City, Missouri. I remember the unfortunate experience of having an Old Testament professor named Ralph Elliot who did not believe the Old Testament record he was teaching me. The next controversy I remember would be over his book and the authenticity of the Biblical record.

By the '70s, I remember reading an article by the executive secretary of the Northwest Baptist Commission of Southern Baptists, in which he stated that fully 50% of the churches in the Northwest were being torn apart by the Charismatic Controversy. Then came Neo-Orthodoxy and the battle for inerrancy. It was a battle that needed to be fought; truth must always be defended. I was a part, and I am grateful. Today all six of our Southern Baptist seminaries are conservative.

Next came the issue over women deacons and women in ministry. Then, could professors teach as they will and still be called Baptists; further, could Baptist press, specifically Broadman Holman and now LifeWay, publish books and print things that would not be consistent with predominant Southern Baptist belief. Of course there was stem cell, abortion, homosexuality and other issues on which Southern Baptists stood right.

One of the greatest battles rages today over the issue of contemporary music. It is one that will be addressed in a subsequent chapter, and which may well settle the battle, at least in your own church.

Now there is Calvinism, no longer a Protestant or a Presbyterian issue, but now the hot new issue among Southern Baptists. Recently, a controversy arose over whether Southern Baptist international missionaries could be appointed who acknowledged they spoke in tongues in a private prayer language. We have recently amended the "Baptist Faith and Message" to be more distinct about women in ministry and the ongoing controversy about the submissive wife. But I must say, Calvinism is hurting us far more than we dare acknowledge.

Every state evangelism conference I preach at has something like 10 to 20% attendance of what it used to be. I was recently in a major southern state preaching their evangelism conference where I spoke regularly 20 years ago. There were always 2,000 and more. Now there are 200, and they are mostly white-haired. The truth of the matter is, our young men are discouraged, disinterested and disillusioned, and it does not bode well for the future of the Southern Baptist Convention.

Recently Jim Draper wisely called a meeting of young leaders to encourage them in denominational participation. The truth of the matter is that virtually all of the students I am teaching in my adjunct professor role at Southwestern Baptist Theological Seminary in Houston are not going into traditional churches. They are starting their own new churches. They simply refuse to get into the battle over the deacon versus pastor leadership controversy and the contemporary versus traditional music worship wars, etc.

And now there is the issue of the emerging church—how to do church, how to dress, what about the music—but more importantly, the message. I think it is essential to remember that the methods may be changing, but the message is worth fighting for and must never change. But somehow, we have become so caught up in consistent controversy that we have lost so very much, and it is hurting us more than we can know.

The October 2007 edition of SBC LIFE carried two important articles. LIFEWAY President Thom S. Ranier said "I'm not saying avoid substantive issues and the calls for accountability, but I plead with my brothers and sisters in Christ, particularly in our denomination, to move toward a more civil discourse, a more Christ-like attitude in what we say and write."

"My passionate desire is to be a bridge builder in the Southern Baptist Convention. Not to compromise biblically. Not to be soft in my theology. I desire true collaboration with those of uncompromising biblical certitude to reach a lost world with the Gospel of our Savior. My prayer is that the conservative resurgence will now grow into a Great Commission resurgence."

"But our witness is compromised when a spiritually lost world sees us fighting with one another, when they see unloving words hurled without restraint, when they see terse comments cloaked in civility—when they see little evidence of Christian love."

Further, Convention President Frank Page wrote, "Our witness is being diluted and energies expanded on other activities, especially on internecine conflict."

"Church conflict is rampant. Seldom does a day go by that I do not receive a call for help from either a church, a pastor, or a staff member. Recently I received three in one day. And there seems to be a new way to deal with church conflict. These days, increasing numbers of church members launch Web sites detailing allegations, accusations, and complaints. I ask church members this question: Do you think lost people see this? When newspaper reporters are called and church conflict becomes known in the newspaper, either locally or nationally, what do you think this does when lost people read it? For Christ's sake, for the sake of the lost, stop!"

A recent article by J. Robert White, Executive Director of the Georgia Baptist Convention said, in part, "As believers who are often at odds with one another, we find ourselves shooting each other while the world around us is dying, lost and condemned without Jesus Christ. Frankly, the only way to have peace in this environment is to have it through a life of deep, personal devotion to Christ." He continues, "I do not have the capacity to understand those who have made the conscious, personal choice to spend their lives and influence attacking and undermining Southern Baptist missions, ministries, and money. I see people I believe to be Christians who are angered by the conservative resurgence in the Southern Baptist Convention and decided during those years that whatever happened they would spend the rest of their days fighting Southern Baptists. What is wrong with this? Satan is what is wrong with this. This is not righteous indignation. This is unrighteousness. The angst is not isolated to disputes between moderates and conservatives, now we have a variation of conservatives that are at war with each other over some very surprising issues such as alcohol and how we will support missions and the degree to which we will support Southern Baptist missionaries. It is time for all of us to get a grip."

As I write these words, I am less than 24 hours removed from attendance at the 2007 Southern Baptist Convention in San Antonio. The San Antonio Express News said yesterday, in an article by J. Michael Packard, "The nation's largest non-Catholic religious party must spend as much passion on lost souls as it does on its internal squabbles, its leader told 8300 messengers Tuesday in San Antonio." He continued, "Half the church has built its own version of the Maginot Line—a supposedly impregnable line of fortifications France built on its border with Germany after World War I which later became a symbol of French defeat when Nazi Germany conquered France in 1940. As French generals trusted in the Maginot Line to save their country from invasion and sent their troops elsewhere, Page said (referring to the presidential address by Dr. Frank Page of First Baptist Taylors, South Carolina), "Southern Baptists have built magnificent churches and wonderful agencies but then fought each other over non-essential issues. We've not been right before God; we've been fighting the wrong battle." While we justly criticize ourselves in an attempt to self-correct from time to time; sadly, the great damage is done by those who observe the battle and ridicule us. The world, you see, does not read Christ, does not read the Bible; it reads us, and they love to see us fight. Oh that we could do so, if we must, at least behind closed doors.

The morning the convention opened in San Antonio, newspaper columnist Roddy Stinson addressed the coming of Southern Baptists to the convention with these headlines in a commentary: "SOUTHERN BAPTISTS ARE CONVENING; WILL ANY CHRISTIANS BE WITH THEM?" "Nineteen years ago, this is how I described the bosses of the Southern Baptist Convention as the nation's largest Protestant denomination began its 1988 convention in San Antonio. Mostly male, mostly white, self-styled 'anointed ones' who control the Southern Baptist Convention and who by the force of their egocentric personalities and their threat of eternal damnation to anyone who opposes them rule and reign as surely—and at times as ruthlessly—as any religious cabal of the Middle Ages (that was one of my nicer descriptions as I prepared the residents of San Antonio for the Baptist invasion)." He continued, "Southern Baptists float from city to city, cutting off ears, punching noses, cracking spines and giving a huge black eye to the Christian faith while proclaiming that God is Love." And this: "If the Southern Baptist Convention was the mafia, resolution of the ongoing war would be easier—and more humane. One half would rub out the other half and get on with the rest of their lives." And this: "This war and the Southern Baptist Convention is simply a big Preacher Fight—an internecine battle to see who gets to be the top dogs, the head honchos, the distributor of the Religious Spoils." Sadly, this disillusioned man not only misjudges us but also is too spiritually immature to know that he does greater damage to the cause of Christ to do so on the front pages of a world-class newspaper than those who are before God, struggling to find answers. The bottom line is this: For 55 years I have been in Christian ministry. From age 18 until 73, I do not recall a time that my denomination has not been battling—and that, in public—over something. And now, as stated of course, there is the ongoing issue of Calvinism, music, preaching, prayer language and so forth.

The convention from which I just returned was both good and bad, both a blessing and troubling. The sermons I heard were wonderful. From the pastor's conference to the president's address to the annual sermon, there was one of the most heart-felt pleas for a return to the priority of Jesus, soul winning, the purity of the Gospel, evangelism and world missions I think I have ever heard. The sad part is, once leaving the auditorium and going back to the real world where we live, it appears that absolutely nothing stuck and made any difference. For two years Bobby Welch traveled the country as president, pleading for a million souls. Sadly this year, we reported a decline in baptisms. And that is what I experienced at the convention; tremendous inspiration and encouragement, but once we left the auditorium, it was as though it never happened.

I sat in the lobby of hotels chatting with messengers. I ate dinner and lunch and breakfast with friends. I talked in the hallways with old acquaintances, and in every case not one word was said about one thing that was preached. Everything was about Calvinism, voting, squabble, and even worse, power struggles for control. I heard endless discussion on the old guard and the new guard; the old heads struggling to hang on to leadership and the new bloggers who are vowing it will not happen. With nothing short of an old-fashioned Holy Ghost revival in which God rends the heavens and tears our hearts from A to Z, I see no hope that anything is going to change. If I attend another Southern Baptist Convention 20 years from now, I see nothing on the horizon to make me believe that anything will be different. There will be new issues, new struggles for power and leadership, ongoing sermons to inspire us to soul-winning, to preaching the priority of Jesus and to fulfilling the great commission, with little happening to bring it about.

Yes, there are good signs. We are winning lost people to Christ. More missionaries are on the international field than ever before. More money is given to the cooperative program and more to the Lottie Moon Christmas Offering for International Missions than in our history. But is it translating into what it's all about—the fulfilling of the Great Commission? Are more people coming to know Christ? Apparently not. 80% of the churches in America are plateaued or declining, and that includes Southern Baptists. 19% are growing because they're swapping members. 1% are growing because they're making converts. And while we are losing a young generation, fully one-third of Southern Baptist churches baptized absolutely no young people last year.

We talk a good game about revival, hearing from Heaven and the outpouring of the Holy Spirit; and we spend three or four minutes in silent prayer at the convention, and that is wonderful. But let me tell you the truth. There will be no revival in the Southern Baptist Convention—no impact on a dying world in which every statistic is virtually getting worse—until Southern Baptists can find a way that control, controversy, criticism and power struggles lie dead in the water, buried at the foot of the cross, and plead with God for revival no matter what the cost to any individual agenda, program or initiative. Until that happens, we're whistling in the dark and rearranging the furniture on the deck of the Titanic.

It breaks my heart to ask the question, but someone must confront the issue. Could God's anointing be withdrawn from the Southern Baptist Convention? The next chapter will speak about the absolute essential of unity. If we are characterized in the eyes of the public as a squabbling, fighting denomination, whether it is caricature or reality, then Jesus' appeal to us that there must be unity in order that the world may believe He came from God is going to see a sad, sad end. I do not have the answer except every ego, every priority, every bit of pride, every self-serving and every agenda-promoting entity in Southern Baptist life must be nailed to the cross; and truly, we talk about nothing, preach about nothing and promote nothing except the purity of the Gospel, the reality and power of Jesus Christ and the Great Commission. And there is time, but God will never bless this convention as He could in spite of all our sermons, programs, challenges and inspirational messages until real revival comes. And that will not happen until somehow we find a way to change not only the image but also the essence of the Southern Baptist Convention I have known for 55 years.

Chapter 2

Unity in the Body

In Matthew 6:13-19, Jesus teaches us how to pray. You know this beautiful passage and have probably known it from childhood. "Our Father which art in Heaven, Hallowed be Thy Name"—so often called the Lord's Prayer; so revered, and yet rather misnamed. This is, in fact, not the Lord's Prayer, but the model prayer. It is not the prayer the Lord prayed, it is the one He taught us to pray and left as a model. The true Lord's Prayer, the intercessory prayer, the one Jesus prayed in the garden for us, is recorded in John, Chapter 17. Go straight to verse 20 to find the key to the Lord's prayer for us. He says, "I do not pray for these alone, but also for ALL THOSE WHO WILL BELIEVE IN ME THROUGH THEIR WORD." In verse 9 He begins by saying, "I pray for them." He is praying for the disciples who are with Him hearing Him pray in their presence. But He is also praying for everyone who will ever become a disciple, for all of those who will ever know Him and believe on Him through the word of those disciples who prayed with Him that night. They won some, who won some, who won others, on down through history, who eventually won our grandparents, who won our parents, who won us. So, for 2,000 years, Jesus has been seated at the right hand of the Father interceding for us to this very hour. And what is His prayer for His church? His heartfelt intercession for His people contains some surprising information. Let us analyze just a bit of it.

THE FIRST THING Jesus prayed for, in verse 3, is "that they may know You." To know Christ simply means to be in union with Him. Knowing Him is a Biblical word for salvation. It is the lovely word that expresses the consummate union of two. Adam KNEW his wife, and she conceived and brought forth a son. Cane and Abel KNEW their wives, and children were born. Mary, discovering she was with child, said, "How can this be, seeing I KNOW not a man?" Jesus said in Matthew 7, "Many will come before Me in judgment in that day and say Lord, didn't we do many wonderful works?" He will say, "Depart from me, I never KNEW you (I was never intimately one with you)." To know about Christ with a head knowledge is one thing; salvation is knowing him intimately and personally—Christ in you and you in Christ—and that is quite another.

THE SECOND PRAYER Jesus prays for them and for us to this very hour is that the Father will keep us. Verse 11 says, "Holy Father, keep, through Your Name, those whom You have given Me." I find it a bit strange on the surface that Jesus would appear to be attempting to persuade the Father to keep His children in eternal security. But one must ask, for whose benefit was this prayer made? Was it for ours, lest the Father would not keep us saved? Was it in our behalf, because we might become lost if He did not convince the Father to keep us in salvation—in eternal security? No, I think not. This prayer was not for our benefit; it was for their benefit—those few disciples who were with Him in the garden in His immediate presence and who heard Him pray. They had seen Judas commit suicide. They saw him fall. They assumed he had fallen from salvation. They assumed he was lost. And they were rather certain that, as hard as it was when Jesus was with them, now that He was leaving, surely it would be even harder. If Judas couldn't make it when Jesus was with him, how could they be expected to make it when He was gone? They were truly shaken at Jesus' words that He would soon be going back to the Father, and they would see Him no more. Hard enough with Him, how hard would it be without Him?

But Jesus was not praying for our security or benefit, He was doing so for their benefit. He had no doubt the Father would keep them secure. His blood was all-sufficient, and the Holy Spirit would seal those who come to Christ and they will always be in eternal security. But they did not know this. Seeing what happened to Judas, they *assumed* that Judas had fallen from salvation and they could as well. The problem is that they did not understand what had happened to Judas. Hear me carefully. Judas did not lose his salvation, for Judas never had it in the first place. Judas was a hypocrite. Jesus explains that to them in the very next verse. "While I was with them in the world, I kept them in Your Name. Those whom You gave Me I have kept, and none of them is lost EXCEPT the son of perdition THAT THE SCRIPTURES MIGHT BE FULFILLED."

Now what did the Scriptures say about Judas that was fulfilled in his "being lost"? The Scriptures said two things of Judas; one, he was a devil from the beginning; and two, he went to his own place. Now where do devils go? Devils go to Hell. Demons are cast into the lake of fire. At that point in history, Judas was the devil incarnate in a man. He was totally demon-possessed, and the devil cannot be saved and then lose his salvation; nor can demons. He was a hypocrite, a phony and a liar from the beginning. JUDAS NEVER HAD SALVATION, AND SO HE COULD NEVER LOSE IT. Those who have it cannot lose it. Those who never had it are in the same category as Judas—hypocrites. Sometimes we see this in church today. People make a profession of faith—we assume they are saved—they return to the world and die in their sins. We assume they lost their salvation. No, they are only hypocrites. They did go to Hell, not because they lost their salvation, but because they never had it in the first place. Judas was a devil from the beginning, and he went to his own place.

Then in what sense did Judas fall? Judas did not fall from salvation; he fell from his bishopric. He fell from his apostolic position. He fell from his position of service in the apostolic band. That is all from which he fell. So Jesus wants the disciples to know, and wants us to know, that he will eternally keep us safe. That prayer was for the disciples' benefit who heard Him pray—which he immediately explained in the following verse—and for ours, as well, today.

Often people will suggest that "If I believed that, I would sin all I want to." Those who truly make such a statement have never been saved. The righteous do not look for excuses to sin. They try to find ways *not* to sin. When a true believer sins, he is sorry; he will repent and be forgiven. He will not continue in sin. Jesus said, "Now are you my disciples IF YOU CONTINUE in My Word." Continuing in His Word does not make us His disciples, it validates that we are. I John and James were both written to say, "By their fruits you shall know them." There are two kinds of faith: genuine saving faith and pseudo-faith (phony or false faith). The difference: it is the nature of saving faith that it endures. If it is real, it will last. If it is not, it will fail, and the individual will, as Judas, end up in Hell. Not because they have lost salvation, but because they never really had it in the first place.

THE THIRD THING Jesus prays for His disciples is that their "joy might be full" (verse 13). Joy is quite different from happiness. Happiness depends on what happens. If things are going well—a raise at work, the kids are doing fine in school—one may be said to be happy. But, to have a deep abiding sense of peace and confidence that all is well—when the marriage is not going well, the kids flunk out of school and the job is lost—this is joy. It is one fruit of the Holy Spirit, and it is one of the great heritages of the child of God—not an absence of trouble and problems but a deep abiding joy in the midst of the problems and in spite of them as well.

THE FOURTH THING Jesus prays is, "Father, protect them" (verse 15). Jesus says, "I do not pray that you take them out of the world, but that you will keep them from the evil one." The definite article "the" means "the one and only." The one and only evil one is the devil. "Father, protect them" from the devil is our Lord's prayer for you. Jesus understands that it's going to be tough down here. We have to live in enemy territory. This is not God's world—not at this juncture of history—the devil is the prince and power of *this* age. The Kingdom of God *was* before time began in Heaven and *will again be* on earth when Christ returns. Until then, the only place the Kingdom of God exists is *within* you. So we live in enemy territory. We live in the kingdom of the devil. We have to work here and witness here and stay here. We are the salt and the light; He needs us, so He leaves us here. But He knows that we are going to be tested, tried, tempted and sometimes tripped up. He prays for our protection: "Father, keep them from the evil one." What a source of comfort and confidence to know that as I live for Christ in this world, He is praying for me every moment that I might be kept from the evil one.

THE FIFTH THING Jesus prays, "Sanctify them" (verse 17). Our Lord understands that, in spite of everything, we will stumble, fall and sin. But we can be made holy again. We can be lifted up, cleansed; we can be sanctified, holified, purified, cleansed once again. And how? By the Word. He says, "Sanctify them by Your Word, Your Word is truth." When we fall and sin, as we remain here as salt and light, we need not remain dirty. We can get clean and holy, get back in the battle, serve our Lord and be His people in a fallen world. Again in verse 19, He emphasizes, "For their sake I sanctify Myself that they also may be sanctified by the truth." Had Jesus not sanctified Himself, kept Himself holy and pure and sinless, He could not have been our sanctification. He would have been a sinner, He Himself would have needed a savior and His blood on the cross would have not been efficacious to save us. He was tempted in all points, as are we. He kept himself holy, perfect, pure and without sin in order that He might be the perfect substitution on Calvary for our sin.

THE SIXTH THING He prays is that we may behold his glory (verse 24). "Father, I desire that they may also, whom you have given me, be with me where I am that they may behold My glory." To this point, only Peter, James and John had beheld His glory on the Mount of Transfiguration. But He wants us to know that there is more. In Heaven, we're all going to behold His glory. I think again, this verse was a promise to His disciples and an encouragement to us, that we might be faithful in our service as we work for Him down here until at last we see Him face to face and behold His glory when He comes and takes us to Heaven.

THE SEVENTH THING is by far the most important in the prayer. In the Greek language, there is little use of adjectives. Seldom do you find something like, "that was the most colossal, stupendous, magnificent, unbelievable, wonderful thing that ever happened." No, that is not the way of the Greek. If the Greek wants to emphasize something, it simply says it again. Now while Jesus prays once that we might know Him, once that we would be kept, that we would have joy, protection, sanctification and ultimately behold His glory, please note that He prays one thing not once, as each of these, but five times. That's right, FIVE times Jesus prays for one thing. Nowhere else in the New Testament is that true. Nowhere is something re-emphasized by such repetition in a single passage. In the Greek, you simply repeat it over and over again if you want to emphasize its importance. Again, think of that, six times he prays for one thing each. But when He comes to the seventh thing—the completion thing, the perfect thing—he prays it FIVE times. Is there any question in your mind that he was saying THIS is important? And what does He pray? He prays for our UNITY.

Notice that it is not for uniformity, for we are all different. The body of Christ is created by unity in diversity. We don't all have the same gifts, same attributes; we're all different, but we're all one; we don't argue, and we're not divisive. A body has many parts—different parts. There is no uniformity in the body, but there is unity. A tree has roots, a trunk, bark, limbs, leaves and fruit; there is no uniformity in a tree, but there is unity. Just so in the beautiful diverse body of Christ, in the local church and across the nation and the world. It is in our unity and diversity that recreates the body of Christ. Note the five times Jesus pleads with the Father that we might be one:

Verse 11— *"that they may be ONE as we are"*
Verse 21a— *"that they all may be ONE"*
Verse 21b— *"that they all may be ONE in us"*
Verse 22— *"that they may be ONE just as we are one"*
Verse 23— *"that they may be made perfect in ONE"*

Think of it. Five times did Jesus emphasize, not our security, not our holiness, not our joy, but our unity. Why is unity to be the absolute priority of the Church as Jesus so clearly states? The answer is in verse 21, "That they all may be one, as you Father are in Me and I in You; that they also may be one in Us, THAT THE WORLD MAY BELIEVE THAT YOU HAVE SENT ME."

The unity of the body is everything. How so? The world does not read the Bible. The Bible is the record of what Jesus said and did and what it means. But the world doesn't believe the Bible; they don't see Jesus. But oh, dear friend, they read us! Nothing, but nothing, but nothing, presents an ugly caricature of Jesus—that distorts the real and makes Him the laughingstock—like perpetual fighting, squabbling and division among His people. When a church fights—when the people argue and split—believe me, by 9:00 the next morning, after the raucous business meeting, it's the subject in every barbershop, beauty shop, grocery store, garage and class-room in town. Oh, look at the Christians fight! The world loves it, because it discredits God's Son and God's Word through us and gives them the freedom to de-authenticate the claims of Christ over their lives and perpetuate their sin. And that's just what they love. Rather than presenting a beautiful, attractive body of Christ that draws people to Him who said "If I be lifted up, I will draw all men unto Me," fighting and squabbling among God's people repulses the world as it presents an ugly caricature of Christ, and men are driven away. Let a church fight, squabble and split, and I promise you it can take 20 years until the next generation grows up that never heard about that split to get your witness back in the community. How many of our churches in the Southern Baptist Convention are named "New Harmony?"

Why is the unity of the people of God essential to the world believing in Him? Before I answer that, I want you to think for a moment about what Jesus just said. THE WITNESS OF THE CHURCH, THE EVANGELISTIC MISSIONARY TESTIMONY WITNESS OF THE CHURCH OF THE LORD JESUS CHRIST, IS INEXTRICABLY BOUND UP IN AND INSEPARABLY ONE WITH ITS UNITY. How so?

There are many analogies used in Scripture to illustrate the rela-tionship of Jesus and His people. He is called the Vine and we the branches. He is the Groom, we the bride. He is the Captain, we the soldiers. He is the Lord, we the servants. But there is none more meaningful than this: He is the Head, we are the body. As the Head in Heaven, Jesus flows his character, His personality, His life, and His very being by the Holy Spirit through His body on earth—His people.

The church—the people of God—is the body of Christ. There are at least three expressions of that body: the local body, the New Testament church; the area/national body, a denomination; and the worldwide body of Christ. Where a church is in harmony with itself; when the people of God get together; each in honor preferring one another; each considering the other more important than himself; each different, though one in Christ; each with no priority, willing to lay aside every issue and sacrifice every possession, "THAT JESUS CHRIST MIGHT BE KNOWN"; a miracle occurs. In that spirit, a kind of perpetual ongoing incarnation of Jesus, happens. Jesus now reveals Himself in a new body, a bigger body, a greater body. When He was in one place in this world, He had tremendous charm and charisma. Women adored Him, little children crawled all over Him, men would die for Him, people struggled to be near Him. His charm was powerful, but now He's gone, and we're here alone. Or are we? The disciples didn't understand, and they were shaken. "Lord, it's going to be terrible without you; we can't make it." Then Jesus said a very astounding thing. "These works that I do shall you do and greater, because I go to My Father and send the Holy Spirit." In essence Jesus said, "Not only is it going to be okay, it's going to be better than it was, because I'm gone and the Holy Spirit comes." How so? When Jesus was on this earth, He was only in one body in one place at one time. But now He's back in a new body, a bigger body, a greater body. Now He incarnates Himself in a body that is larger, wider, and potentially even capable of greater works than when He was here. When He was in one body, He was limited to one time, one place. But now, because He has come back invisibly in the person of the Holy Spirit, He incarnates Himself in a bigger body that is capable of doing even more—obviously not greater in quality, but greater in quantity because there are more of us. That is why we must absolutely protect the unity of the body of Christ.

Am I saying we must compromise and sweep issues under the table? Not at all. I am saying that the spirit with which we discuss issues must never be done in a self-serving, power-seeking manner. Paul said, "In honor, preferring one another, let each consider the other more important than himself." How powerful is that? I may not agree with you, but in love, I'm going to fight harder for you to be heard and your opinion respected than I am for my own opinion to be accepted. When we lay down our lives for one another; when unity is our priority; when we have no issue but Jesus Christ, His lordship, His deity, His will, and His glory; then the reality of Christ attracts people by the thousands rather than repels them.

When I preached in view of a call at First Baptist Church of Houston in 1970, many people walked out at 12:00. They weren't mad. They came back that night and voted for me. They had just been going home at 12:00 for years. Now today, when we *do* let them out, they won't go home. They just stand around and hug each other; they don't want to leave. And the most consistent comment I heard about our church through 30 years was "I just can't wait 'til Sunday." What made the church so attractive? Why do people stand in line to get in and scramble for seats—can't wait to get there and won't leave when they do get there? It is because they're in the presence of Jesus Christ recreated in a new body through the unity of His people. Unity is everything.

I don't profess to have all the answers. There are serious issues that must be dealt with. But we must find new ways to never be self-serving, self-seeking, cantankerous, belittling or critical to the degree that the world writes articles about us in which they see nothing of Jesus and everything of our squabbles. In that, we can destroy our witness. We can tear ourselves apart as a denomination, as a body of Christ, and perhaps even more important, as a local church.

Everything is not addressed in the New Testament—what time your services should be, who should be the new pastor, what kind of music you will have, whether to relocate the church. There are things the people of God must decide. How do we do so? God speaks through His body. We meet, we pray, we talk; we express our views in honor, love and respect; and then we vote. Once the vote is taken, we must assume that Christ has expressed His will as the Head in Heaven through His body on earth. If you cannot live with that, then you need to bite your tongue, move down the street and join another church. But you *cannot* and *must not* tear up the fellowship and divide the church of which you are a member. Once the majority has spoken, Christ has spoken through His people. END OF STORY! Unity in the church, in the denomination and in the world—as much as is possible—is greatly to be sought.

My first Sunday in Houston, I walked through the nurseries and the preschool and found five or six children. Today there are more like 700 or 800. Young couples are coming in droves. Our new pastor, Gregg Matte, is being mightily used of God, in his grace and humility and faithfulness to the Word, to win people to Christ in an unprecedented manner. First Baptist Church is booming; people are pouring in. They come early, and they stay late. And to their credit, my deacons still understand and practice the priority of deaconship in being a protector of the fellowship at all costs.

May God help us, in gentleness and grace, to find ways to prioritize the purity of the Gospel and the glory of Jesus Christ, to the end that people will be drawn to Him, in our lives and homes, in our churches and in our denomination. In Jesus' name, Amen.

Chapter 3

The Question of Elder Rule

Throughout the years, I have had the reputation of being a friend of pastors. It is one that is justly deserved; I do indeed love preachers. Because of that, uncounted times my phone has rung with a preacher on the other end struggling over an issue, asking for consultation and advice. Not surprisingly, 95% of calls were about the same problem—conflict between pastor and deacons over authority and leadership in the church. Because of this, many Southern Baptist pastors are over-reacting and going the other way, seriously examining the issue of Elder Rule—a system in which just a few, perhaps three, seven, 10 or 12 make all the decisions and "run" the church. If you are starting a new church or planning a new ministry, this might work. But to attempt to change the position of leadership held by deacons in traditional Southern Baptist churches is generally a fatal mistake and one that may cost you your ministry. And it is not necessary. The problem is *not* that we need a new system; the problem is that we need to understand why the system we already have does not work. And it is a constant ongoing struggle. Few churches have escaped the nightmare of deacons and pastor conflict over leadership and authority in the church. Jesus is the Head in Heaven, and His body on earth is intended to function smoothly, in unity and in harmony. Division at the top level is usually fatal. How sad when it can be so easily remedied.

Certainly none of us have all the answers and know everything about how to perfectly administer the work of the Lord in a New Testament church. There is disagreement; and oftentimes, different systems work fairly well. But let's examine what we do know from Scripture.

First of all, we know that the pastor is the undershepherd, the leader of the church. In the Ephesians 5 passage where Paul speaks about a wife submitting herself to her husband, honoring him as the head of the home, he says, "I speak of Christ and the church." But examined in context, it is clear that there is a kind of mutual submission inherent in this relationship. In Ephesians 5:21, the controversial passage on the submissive wife begins in context with an admonition to "Submit yourselves one to another." There is a mutual submission of selfless serving of the other that brings about a harmonious relationship in the home and in the church. In short, the husband is not gaining his leadership by demanding it and bullying his wife. He deserves it; he earns it; he wins it by honoring her, pouring out his life for her in ministry and service. Every decision is made on the basis of "How can I honor and bless and exalt my precious wife?" What woman would not be only too happy to honor her husband as the head of the home who relates to her in this manner? In the same way, a church must honor their pastor as the leader, the undershepherd, of the church. But he too must earn that position. It must indeed be granted by the congregation, but earned by the pastor.

Even our Lord was the example as a servant leader for us. He requires our loyalty and honor and obedience, but He went to the cross, poured out His life for us and earned it and deserved it by dying for us. When Paul writes the church at Ephesus, he says, "Wives, submit yourselves to your husbands," then adds "and husbands, honor your wife, and serve her as Christ did the church." And how did Christ love the church? He died for her. The submission, the service, the humility of the husband to his wife is in a sense even greater than hers to him. She is not told to die for him, he is told to die for her, to love her as Christ did the church and died for it. So, for a pastor to be the leader of the church, the undershepherd for the Upper Shepherd, he must earn that position, and it must be granted by the congregation as well. And what congregation would not be only too happy to honor that pastor as the head of the church, the earthly leader, when he is pouring out his life in ministry and service selflessly for his people as Christ did the church and as the husband is to do for the wife?

Many terms are used to describe the pastor of a congregation. And they are used interchangeably in the New Testament. He is the gift of God to the church in I Corinthians. In Revelation, he is the angel of the church. He is also called pastor, shepherd, overseer, bishop and elder. All of these are terms for the same position. How does a pastor earn the leadership the Bible teaches and the church must grant? There is no question that he is the earthly leader of the congregation, the undershepherd leading the congregation to follow the Upper Shepherd, Jesus the Head in Heaven; but pragmatically, how is he to do so? Many ingredients go into becoming the man of God who earns and deserves the title pastor and undershepherd.

His leadership, first of all, is earned by humility. He is reminded in I Peter 5 not to lord it over God's heritage. He is to be an example to the flock. Humility is always required for those who will become first as leader. Never forget "The last shall be first," and "He that is greatest among you must be servant of all." So the pastor of the congregation must earn that leadership by his humility.

Secondly, he earns it by service to the people. He pours out his life to them in ministry. He visits them; he cares about them. He is a compassionate and tender shepherd who ministers selflessly to the needs of the congregation.

Thirdly, he earns his leadership by feeding the flock. Every time he stands before the congregation to teach or preach, he is to be well-prepared, filled with the Spirit and ready to teach God's Word.

Fourthly, he earns his leadership by integrity. Through the years I have found that only 1 in 10 men who begin their ministry at age 21 are still in it at age 65. Of those that make it "all the way," few are superstars, brilliant preachers or charismatic personalities. They are, however, all men of humility and integrity. God cannot use a sinful man. There must be holiness, honesty, transparency and purity. Certainly there are more ways by which a pastor earns the leadership which the church must grant. But these must be in abundance and must be prominent.

In I Peter 5:1-4, Peter exhorts the elders about how to do their ministry. He says six things about who they are and how they live, but only two specifically about what they are to do. And those two are: "Feed the flock of God which is among you, and take oversight thereof." I take that to mean that someone else in the staff or church can do everything that needs to be done except two—the two things no one can do for me. The first is to study and pray and be prepared to teach and preach God's Word every time I stand before my congregation. The second is to seek the heart of God, point the way and give leadership to the church. These things no one else can do; these things *you* must do, all in the context of humility, ministry, service and integrity called for in the Word of God. So as we look at the question of Elders, let us begin by getting in perspective of who and what the pastor is as well as the deacons in a Baptist church.

For centuries we as Baptists have had a system of church government by which deacons work with the pastor as the ruling body, with the congregation the ultimate authority in matters of major importance. Let's look at the deacons.

If many, if not the majority, of Southern Baptist churches, have from time to time experienced great trauma in the area of deacon-pastor leadership authority, how can it be that such a system exists? Is it possible that this is what the Holy Spirit had in mind when he birthed the church? It is hard for me to believe that a system this flawed at its premise can be what the Spirit intended. That is not to say that pastors and deacons cannot be the leaders of the church. It is not to say we need a new system. It is to say WE NEED TO MAKE THE ONE WE HAVE WORK. Just as the first ingredient is a correct understanding of the pastor's role—earned, not demanded—so is it absolutely essential that deacons come to understand the nature of their role. Again, the system doesn't need to be overhauled, but it certainly needs to be tweaked—with the pastor understanding his role and the deacon understanding his.

In the New Testament, a major contention arose in the church between two groups of women over the distribution of benevolent funds for their daily needs. How terrible! What could be worse than a cat fight in a Baptist church? I have a deep sense that when the disciples said, "Appoint you seven men of good reputation to handle this matter," the purpose of the first deacons was not primarily to administer the business of the church, but rather, to deal with the issue of a broken fellowship within the congregation. This was far more serious than the distribution of bread. Remember our thoughts about the importance of unity. Again, the deacons were not established primarily to do the business administration of the church but to heal the broken fellowship which had been created over the issue. When deacons understand that, when they are committed primarily to protecting the fellowship of the church at any cost, then they rise to a higher level, and just as a pastor earns his position, earn their right to be a part of the leadership of the congregation in the decision-making process. They too must earn their right to lead. A deacon who has this kind of attitude, who is far more concerned about protecting his church than voting on how the church spends its money, is a deacon that will be a blessing.

For 30 years at First Baptist Church of Houston, I had such deacons, and I commend them today. I honor them; their priority was to maintain the fellowship. And I can honestly say that in 30 years, I don't think I had a serious problem. Oh, I'm sure there were problems, but I didn't know about them. The deacons handled them; they took care of them. Where there was criticism, misunderstanding and conflict, they would seek out the folks in the Sunday school class, in the hallways, after the services, in their home and in committee meetings and attempt to be peacemakers, shedding light, solving the problem and protecting the unity. And the church operated in such beauty and harmony, that the body of Christ created the reality of Jesus, and people were drawn in droves—coming early and staying late. This attitude creates a mindset in a deacon that lifts him far above the kind of deacon who often tries to be the church boss, run everything and battle the pastor over leadership.

Imagine a surgeon preparing over the weekend to do Monday morning brain surgery on a four-year-old child. He gathers his surgical team, does the X-rays, the blood tests, prepares himself, gets everything ready and begins to perform the surgery. But just suppose that the four-year-old child is the brain surgeon's little girl or boy. Then he brings to the X-rays, team, operation procedure, and entire process a far different attitude. He is a far better surgeon, because his first priority is the life and safety and comfort of that precious child. When a deacon's priority is not just to gather information, get a team, vie for leadership and push through an agenda; but rather, to protect the fellowship of the church, which is "his little boy, his baby," he brings to the deacon leadership a far different attitude which changes everything.

So church government in the area of leadership, short of those things on which the church actually votes, can be easily resolved without changing the whole system and going to a few men who are elders running everything—if both pastor and deacons are the kind of men described. Rather than changing the system, improve the system you already have, and it will work far better in the average Southern Baptist church.

There are two kind of leadership: participatory and autocratic. Autocratic rule, where one man makes all the decisions, is neither New Testament nor smart. First, no man is that wise. There is indeed much wisdom in many counselors. I lunched recently with one of three men who, along with the pastor, alone make all the decisions in a certain mega-church. I asked, "Does the church ever vote on anything?" and he replied, "No." That dear pastor is probably heading for trouble down the way. Where there is no one but one person in autocratic leadership—or a very tiny handful of two or three in authority—you tend to cultism, you neglect the wisdom of the counsel of people, you forfeit buy-in spiritually, financially and prayerfully from the congregation, and you fail to train leadership in the process. Autocratic rule is fraught with much potential danger.

Participatory leadership is the New Testament way, and it is the best way. Remember: IT DOES NOT MATTER WHAT YOU CALL THEM, YOU NEED A TEAM TO HELP YOU IN LEADERSHIP. You may call them by different names. Some churches call them deacons; others, elders; still others, trustees, the session, leadership team or church counsel. It doesn't matter what you call them. The important thing is that you are not supposed to do it by yourself. He who does not share leadership, solicit the advice of others and is not accountable, will regret it. Our dear friend Jimmy Swaggart fell into sin. The Assemblies of God required him to be submissive for two years to the counsel and accountability of a group of Assemblies of God pastors. Brother Swaggart said, "I'm bigger than the whole Assemblies of God denomination," and refused. Eight months later he fell again, and it was all over.

Before you go to a system of Elder Rule, with five or ten men holding all authority and no one else making any decisions, think about some questions such as: These are the leaders of our church. Says who? Does no one vote on anything? How are they dismissed? Who appoints new men and for how long? My son Tim told me of a fellow pastor in his city who started a church in his home and ran it for 20 years with only himself and three other elders—he being the chief elder—making all the decisions. One day, the other elders fired him! You must have a constitution and by-laws. The by-laws must be well thought out and followed, and they must address the matter of how decisions are made. All of them being made by one man is not good.

There is much of which we cannot be certain about the teaching of elders in the New Testament. We do know that their names are used interchangeably with pastor, shepherd, overseer, bishop and other names. When the apostle Paul addresses the elders and sends Timothy to appoint elders, one cannot be certain whether that is one elder in each church or a plurality of elders in one church. I think we can be sure that the Bible teaches us there is much wisdom in many counselors—and experience has borne out the fatal flaw of auto-cratic leadership—and assume that there were many men who were elders serving by whatever name in each church, while one—the pastor—served as chief elder.

The Dallas Theological Seminary-trained Bible Church pastors have used the elder rule system for many decades. It is almost unheard of to hear about a squabble or fight in a Bible Church. I have spoken with three of their more prominent pastors and professors recently, and they all agree that it is essential that the elders be elected BY the church, are accountable TO the church, rotate, and that the church votes on some things as we shall see in the next chapter. They all emphasize one word: balance—consisting of pastoral leadership, elder board, congregation and committees. But they all said their system works beautifully and smoothly in an atmosphere of "In honor preferring one another, let each consider the other more important than himself." This is the New Testament way. A group of men serving as elders, working with the pastor, as chief elder, to make most decisions as they lead the church with the congregation the ultimate authority voting on some things, as we shall see.

Again remember, it doesn't matter what you call them: deacons elders, the session, trustees, whatever. You need such a group of people, appointed by and accountable to the church, who do not serve in perpetuity. So fellow Baptist pastor, before you change your system of church government, throw out the deacons, dismiss congregational government and move to a system of Elder Rule, you'd better think a long time. It is far better to tweak the system you already have. The deacons I know are good, Godly men who want to do right. Help them to understand their priority, how they earn their leadership—by service and protecting the fellowship. You do the same in your ministry, and you can bring about a balance that is at once sweet and effective in any Baptist Church. Again, it's all about balance between pastor, deacons, committees, and congregations.

The issue of congregation voting is huge, and none of the above will work unless we get it right. Let's look at that.

Chapter 4

You're Voting on What?

Nothing can be clearer in the New Testament than that a congregational form of church government is the Biblical pattern. We shall see clearly that the church expressed its collective opinion in many matters. Certainly, many things are clear in the New Testament and need no vote. Where the Bible speaks, simply do it. But there are hundreds of decisions made in the life of the church that are not covered in the New Testament. Whom shall we call as our next pastor? Will we have a youth camp this summer? Shall we relocate? Is the church budget sufficient for another year? What about changing the name of church or borrowing a large sum of money for a building program? Certainly, someone needs to decide these things.

The question becomes, who decides what in a Baptist Church? Some years ago, one of our deacons questioned my authority to make a certain decision. I said to all the deacons, "Brothers, there are probably over a hundred decisions a day made around this church. We have seven major ministries, a school, an eight-million dollar budget and a hundred staff members. And every decision that we make relates to some committee. If you wish, I can call a hundred committee meetings a day and none of you would ever get anything done at your job. Or, we can assume that we have a competent staff; men and women called of God, who are skilled in their field, who know how to make decisions, who are not spiritual noo-noos and can act. We also have a pastor who is not a novice and can make decisions. Now obviously there are certain things that need to be voted on by the church. And things of that importance will always be brought to you for counsel and support first." But the question then becomes, at what level are decisions made? The staff makes decisions, the pastor makes decisions, committees make decisions, deacons make decisions and the church makes some decisions. "Now we have a nightmare situation trying to unscramble who does what. So I want to ask you for one year to give me the authority to be the man who makes the decisions as to who makes the decisions. After one year, I want you to review it and tell me how it's working." Six years later, no one had said anything. The church was operating smoothly, so I brought the issue up once again and asked how they thought the system was working with the pastor making the decision as to at what level decisions would be made. And they said, "Oh, Pastor, it's working just fine. Keep it up." This then becomes where the rub comes in. I would say that through the years, my staff made most all the decisions. Generally, if we needed to hire a new custodian, the Building Superintendent simply hired him. If it was a matter of hiring an outside firm to do all the cleaning, that would be of significance that the Properties Committee would need to be involved. If there was to be a youth rally, I simply gave the Youth Director the responsibility to organize it, advertise it and put it on. No vote was needed. The Music Director and I visited regularly about the music for the services, and with a broad amount of latitude, he chose the music, and we were all pleased and blessed with the result. So mostly, the staff made the decisions.

Now, occasionally there would be decisions that were of such importance that the staff came to me for input or even the final decision. We made those decisions collectively at staff meetings about three hours a week, every Tuesday morning. Additionally, my door was always open for them. I made most of my major decisions in consultation with my staff and other appropriate leadership. Sometimes, I would simply go to the staff and say "Here's what we're going to do" and give them a directive. So certainly I made some decisions. Our people learned to trust me and trust the staff, and that trust is a key element of making the system work. And remember the ingredients for trust: feeding the flock, ministering to the people, humility, integrity and longevity.

Committees are of great value. As you use committees, you train leadership. During our 4-1/2 year interim the First Baptist Church grew without a pastor. The reason? Great leadership. The leaders had been developed by giving them a chance to lead. It was not uncommon for me to go to a committee and say, "Here's an issue we're struggling with, that we need to think through. I want you all to talk about it and let me know what you decide." Committees, pastor and staff all make decisions, but at some point things rise to a level of significance in which the deacons need to be consulted and their wisdom and support enlisted. These kinds of decisions can normally be made at a monthly deacon's meeting, without having to call a special meeting. In a Baptist Church, deacons serve as the elder board and are appointed by the church which looks to them for shared leadership with the pastor. I've never talked to my deacons about an important decision, that we did not refine it and come out with a better decision. They too are good men. They have wisdom, their counsel is important; and together, we can do a better job than any of us can do alone. Sometimes I defer to them, sometimes they to me. But the great majority of the time, we massaged an issue until we came to the best decision, and we did so together.

At that juncture, you then decide, does the issue rise to a level of significance such that the church must approve it? It is there that the rub comes in. Let me say frankly that perhaps the curse of little churches is that they want to vote on everything. Conversely, it is just as bad—if not worse—that big churches far too often vote on nothing. Neither of these things are New Testament. In a smoothly functioning New Testament church, people must learn to trust each other and allow pastor, staff and committees to make decisions; being certain that if something is of real importance, it will be brought before the deacons and ultimately voted on by the church. The great heartache that I have observed in small churches is the tendency for everyone wanting to know everything about everything, and vote on everything. Put this in your heart and preach it to your people: the more you vote and discuss matters publicly, the more chance you open the door to controversy, division and loss of testimony due to the declining unity of the church. VOTE ON AS LITTLE AS POSSIBLE. Only the big things should be discussed publicly. More about that in a moment.

But again, the heartache of so many small churches is the tendency for everyone to vote on everything. In the deacon's meeting at my first pastorate, one of the deacons raised the question, "Why are we already fourteen dollars over the budget for light bulbs for the year, when we're only three or four months into the new year?" When I arrived at the church a few weeks earlier, the church was very dark, and I asked the custodian to install new larger light bulbs to brighten the auditorium. This had "blown the budget" for the whole year. Can you imagine that? The world is perishing, and deacons are spending their time discussing fourteen-dollar expenditures for light bulbs. But I find this to be a recurring problem in small churches. In all honesty, generally, larger churches do not fight as much as small churches. I think the reason is that people in large churches learn to trust each other. They expect to be involved less in the decision-making process of the day-by-day smaller decisions; they expect others to make them. And they do. And it works smoothly. But they do know that the church is going to vote on some things. I urge you to attempt to move your church towards a philosophy where the church votes on only a few large matters. There are those who make fun of churches voting, and not only ridicule it but actually go to the extreme of never voting on anything. This is not New Testament; this is not Biblical.

In the New Testament, the church acted together to decide several things. Let's examine a few of them, remembering that where God speaks clearly on stated issues already in Scripture, we are to act upon them; no further action is needed. But there are many issues not covered in the Scripture, which someone must decide. In the New Testament, the church decided on some issues; but keep clearly in mind, ONLY THE BIGGEST QUESTIONS. The major issues always included the multitude. Don't go to the extreme of not deciding on anything collectively.

In the Upper Room the church existed in its earliest form, though it was not technically called the church until the Day of Pentecost. But the church did exist before Pentecost with those 120 disciples meeting in the Upper Room. They had a decision to make. Judas had committed suicide, fallen from his position of service in the apostolic band and was no longer a disciple. Who was to be his replacement? They discussed it, prayed and cast lots. Acts 1:26 says, the "lot" fell on Matthias. I have wondered if, ironically, the first church decision was not a mistake, because we never hear from Matthias again. But then I began to understand that the apostle Paul, who was GOD'S choice for the twelfth apostle, was not yet even converted, as we see in the following chapters. So, just because we do not hear from him again, it may well be that Matthias served faithfully—though only for a brief time—until the Holy Spirit replaced him with God's choice: the apostle Paul. The point is, they acted collectively. They determined their leaders. Remember that. That's the first principle. The church acted on a major issue: who would be their twelfth disciple.

Then they determined another kind of servant leader, and that was the deacons. In Acts, Chapter 6, they congregationally expressed their will. The whole church chose the seven men named as the first deacons. In Acts, Chapter 6 again, it was the church collectively who made that decision. They were not appointed by the apostles, they were chosen by the multitude as directed by the apostles. So clearly in Acts 1 and Acts 6, the whole church acted collectively in making the big decision in determining their leadership; the twelfth apostle and the deacons.

In Acts, Chapter 10, several people received the Spirit of Christ, were born again, and the question was raised to the congregation — to the multitude: "Can any man 'forbid water' seeing these have received the Holy Spirit as well as we?" They were asking for affirmation, approval and support from the people as to their baptism. So clearly, in Acts 10, the people determined who would be admitted to the fellowship. "Does anyone know anything we don't know? Do you approve this? Let's make this decision together. It's far too serious for one person to decide." And so the congregation approved the administration of water baptism, and they became part of the New Testament fellowship.

In Matthew, Chapter 18, another kind of church vote is inferred in the New Testament. Jesus tells the simplest form of a local church, where two or three are gathered together, how to deal with discipline regarding a sinning brother. He is to be sought out individually, then with a few, and if still unrepentant, brought before the church, not with a view of discipline, but with a view of confession, forgiveness and restoration. But what happens when the man refuses to repent? Then he is to be DISMISSED FROM THE FELLOWSHIP. And Jesus said, "Whatever decision you make in this matter on earth as My body, I, as the Head of Heaven, will back up and support." So clearly, in Acts 10, the church decided who would be admitted to the fellowship; and in Matthew 18, who would be dismissed from the fellowship. These two issues as well as the selection of leaders—two huge matters—were determined by the New Testament church collectively.

In Acts 15, there remains at least one other time the church acted congregationally. The controversy that arose over the issue of whether Gentile believers had to be circumcised to become Christians was so sharp, it was referred to the Jerusalem Counsel where all the elders and all the apostles gathered together to discuss it and make a decision. Now this was doctrinally the most important issue the church ever dealt with in the New Testament. Please note that this huge controversial important issue was dealt with by the whole church. Let's examine Acts 15. In verse 3, Paul and Barnabas make their journey to Jerusalem to discuss the issue with the larger group, and they were sent by the church. In verse 4, when they arrived in Jerusalem, they were received by the church—the whole church—and the apostles and elders. In verse 7, Peter arose and said, "Men and Brethren." This expression is always used when the entire larger congregation is being addressed. It is a public gathering, well beyond a meeting between the disciples and elders; it is a meeting with the whole church. In verse 12, all the multitude kept silent as Barnabas and Paul began to speak. In verse 13, James then stood and addressed the same congregation—the same men and brethren. Clearly, the conversation, the discussion, the debate is going on before the entire church. And it was apparently a very large congregation.

In verse 22, "Then it pleased the apostles and elders WITH THE WHOLE CHURCH" to send Paul, Barnabas, Judas Barsabas and

Silas on to the rest of the churches in Asia Minor to tell them the decision that had been made, which was that Gentiles did not have to be circumcised to be Christians and be part of the church. Verse 23 says, "They wrote letters by them." They wrote the letter and they sent the letter at the hand of the apostles. By whom? Again, verse 23, "THE APOSTLES, THE ELDERS AND THE WHOLE CHURCH." To whom did they send it? Also in verse 23, "to the brethren." That is, to all the brethren in Antioch, Syria and Cilicia. In verse 30, the people gathered together to hear the decision that had been made by the Jerusalem Counsel. Listen carefully to the 30th verse: "So when they were sent off, they came to Antioch; and when they had GATHERED THE MULTITUDE together, they delivered the letter."

The heartache of small churches is voting on everything. The tragedy and pitfall of large churches can be voting on nothing. The Biblical way is congregationally determining SOME things. The sensible thing is to follow the New Testament pattern and let the church be the ultimate authority in the decision-making process — BUT ONLY IN THE MAJOR ISSUES.

We see three categories acted on in the New Testament which are not necessarily exhaustive; only representative: electing leadership, receiving and dismissing membership, and deciding a major doctrinal issue. Remember that doctrinal issues were new in those days. I do not believe a local New Testament congregation ought to be voting on doctrinal issues today. It is the responsibility of the pastor to articulate the doctrines of the church. If he is not doing so, then let him be dismissed. New Testament doctrine is not up for grabs. The Bible means what it says, and it says what it means. We'll rue the day we start voting on doctrine in our Southern Baptist churches. Surely we know what we believe by now.

What then are those larger things the church should be voting on? Let me answer that by telling you what some churches are doing. Many churches, particularly larger churches in the Southern Baptist Convention, are going back and looking at the by-laws, rewriting some, and trying to identify what they will vote on as a congregation. Most of them have developed a list something like this:

1. Who their leadership will be—pastor, major staff, Sunday school teachers, committee members and deacons.
2. Adoption of the annual church budget.
3. Changes to the by-laws.
4. A major decision like changing the name of the church or relocation.
5. The borrowing of a substantial amount of money.
6. A building program or relocation program.

The purpose of these chapters is to shed some light on some of the more controversial issues before our convention. We must make progress toward unity in our churches and our denomination if our world witness is to be taken seriously. Certainly the issue of Elder Rule is a hot topic among us. Voting on certain things relates very much to Elder Rule as it in turn reflects church leadership and the decision-making process. We're going to be looking at contemporary music, Calvinism, private prayer languages and other hot topics; all with an eye not toward solving everything but certainly giving you the tools with which to make at least some progress in your church toward unity.

Chapter 5

The Battle Over Relevance

Silently, a battle rages in the arena of religion and theology regarding truth. What is truth? For a Christian, it is that which is consistent with the character of God, the self-expression of God in the Word of God. For centuries that definition sufficed. Now, in this postmodern era, it is no longer universally held by all "evangelicals."

Many "emerging church" leaders assert that truth is hazy, indistinct and uncertain—perhaps even ultimately unknowable. Brian McLaren, one of the leaders of the emerging church has stated, "I don't think we have the gospel right yet. None of us has arrived at orthodoxy." Orthodoxy is a covering for harsh, inflexible dictums from an arrogant preacher who is overstating a position. It is also the opinion of many of their leaders that truth is in flux and is impossible to state with certainty on any particular doctrine.

But is that authentic Christianity? Martyrs throughout history have given their lives to proclaim the truth of the Gospel of Christ as revealed in the Bible. The answer to unbelief and apostasy has always been to declare the veracity of the Word of God, the Bible, as our only guide for faith, doctrine and practice. Now, some modern evangelicals are back-peddling and saying that the Bible is so controversial and difficult to understand, we must not argue over trivialities which are not that important anyway. This is a very slippery slope indeed. If we depart from any truth as revealed in the

Scriptures, which ones will survive and which ones shall we teach new believers to believe?

Clearly, the existence of absolute truth and its inseparable relationship to the person of God is the most essential tenet of all true Christianity. And that truth is "fleshed out" in the person of Jesus Christ and accurately recorded in Scripture.

Truth is under attack, and few warriors are willing to engage the enemy on his territory for fear they will appear "too negative," or that certain issues are "merely doctrinal" and therefore not worth the effort. The answer is for Christians who believe the truth of the Gospel and the Bible to "contend earnestly for the faith."

Truth is important. But is it really worth fighting for? Indeed! "The truth shall set you free" has not been annulled by Christ. It is truth that sets the sinner free from sin, condemnation, judgment and hell, and builds up the saint.

Paul called the church "the pillar and ground of truth." If the church will not protect their believers from apostates, who will fight the good fight for the truth of the Gospel? Peter, Paul and Jude spoke of the false prophets active in their day.

IS THE EVANGELICAL CHURCH TODAY CONTENDING FOR THE FAITH? This issue cannot be swept under the carpet. Too much of the emerging church paradigm has come to replace substance.

Evangelicals have historically stood firmly for certain foundational truths that have defined orthodoxy. These include: justification by faith, substitutionary atonement, Christ's deity, His virgin birth and His bodily resurrection. Rather than contending for the faith, many current leaders are more concerned with contending against evangelicals who would dare to state such truth in a dogmatic fashion. Keeping in touch with modern fads seems to be the main program of many in order to gain the approval of our depraved generation.

Removing man-made barriers to come to church is certainly wise, but if evangelical Christians water down their doctrines and truth, they drift into the trap of weakening the very Gospel they are to proclaim and in the process lose their effectiveness with the very people they are trying to reach. The Gospel is still the power of God unto salvation.

One reason that truth is fuzzy is that so many church leaders believe the issues are pliable and therefore open to any and all "doctrines". Some even believe there is room for non-Christian beliefs in this postmodern climate. This is perfectly normal, however, if you understand that an apostate will use any means to continue to hold sway over his followers however repugnant the idea to mainstream orthodoxy.

But the young and unlearned are not the only ones being captured by apostasy. Many church leaders have departed from the faith and are now proclaiming teachings that were not acceptable to most only a few years ago. When lust and greed enter the landscape, the consequences are predictable. The desire for power and recognition are serious motives for apostates to deliver their distorted message to their followers. One merely need look at the new wave of "miracle healers" to understand what is at stake in the new "church". Simon the sorcerer is a prime example of one who hears, believes, is baptized and follows Peter as he continues his miraculous signs. But it is clear from Peter's later statement, "You have neither part nor portion in this matter, for your heart is not right in the sight of God."

Knowing the truth, they depart from it for their own selfish gain. That is the crux of the matter in dealing with false prophets, or apostates. They always look like believers, but enter into willful, deliberate sin. Someone who has not heard the Gospel and makes false claims about salvation and Heaven is not an apostate. Apostates take a kernel of the truth they have heard and twist it to fit their pernicious agenda to manipulate and control people. So an apostate is worse than a simple ignorant proclaimer of false teaching. The apostate is deliberately and knowingly stating "truth" that he knows is diametrically opposed to the Biblical revelation.

These "clouds without water" devote their lives to opposing the ideas they have heard and reject. Their "damnable lies" become fodder for the unlearned from the pig trough of aberrant theology. They "have been there," "I used to believe, before I became enlightened, so let me enlighten you." It sounds too much like the original lie: "Has God not said, 'Listen to me and you shall be as gods.'"

Most of the time serious error can be recognized for what it is, but with modern apostates, the lines become blurred. That is why we must be vigilant, wise and discerning when we hear any new "strange doctrine". Often serious threat comes to our faith through subtle camouflage. And all false teachers surround their lies with some degree of truth or half-truth and confuse and dupe their hearers. Christians can never be certain of a leader if we go only by his charming manner, warm personality or majority opinion regarding his message. The Bible is our sole guide for truth and has always been.

Is the church contending for "The Faith"? Those of us who believe in the inerrant, infallible original manuscripts as handed down by God to Holy men of old must stand in the gap or the gap will become a chasm into which millions will trip and lose their soul.

"For certain men have crept in." —*Jude 4*

Jesus called the promoters of false religion "whitewashed tombs...full of dead men's bones." Most false prophets and charlatans cleverly disguise their message behind half truths in order to gain a following. However, there are men like Jim Jones and David Koresh who spiel their venomous poison openly for the world to observe, depending on their strength of personality and hypnotizing rhetoric. If Jim Jones and David Koresh can gain a following, consider the damage a slick, well groomed, religious salesman can do with guile, deceit and the support of much of the organized church.

Jude spoke of these as "spots in your love feasts" serving only themselves. Can someone like that be more dangerous than an outspoken critic of our beliefs? Absolutely!! The fifth column from the inside has always been more dangerous than the critic taking shots from the outside. In reading Scripture, it is clear that false teachers, apostates, heretics and false prophets were already infiltrating the church in great numbers, hence the many warnings. Like the Judaizers and Gnostics of the days of Paul and Jude, the modern apostates who peddle their spiritual "pig slop" to the young and unlearned clearly clutter up the beauty of the Gospel.

The battle for truth is never ending. Jude mentions the fall of Satan and the angels who followed him. He refers to Adam by name. He mentions the error of Cain. He points to the immorality of Sodom and Gomorrah, the false teaching of Balaam and the rebellion of Korah. He covered all the issues in order that we understand the battle had gone on from nearly the first day of creation to this present hour. Our day mirrors what was happening in Bible days. The similarity could not be more alarming and distinct. The wave of apostasy is rolling into mainstream religion with ever increasing numbers and influence. There is a steady drumbeat of theologians, sport figures, movie stars and influencers who are willing to lend their names to the claims that dispute the clear teaching of the Bible.

One small issue will serve to make the point. The main doctrine of "Oneness Pentecostalism" is the denial of the Trinity. Many in the evangelical camp have glibly parroted the "party line" until there is widespread confusion on this issue, even among some who previously stood firm in the doctrine of the Trinity. TV evangelists, musicians and writers are parading a steady diet of "Oneness" theology through television, movies, music and print media.

"Ungodly men, who turn the grace of our God into lewdness." —
Jude 4

Truth, as revealed by the teaching of Paul and Jude, will also keep us pure. False teachers abound and often play the trump card of immorality for all that it will get them. David Koresh and Jim Jones, as well as many other false prophets, taught that the women and girls in their compounds should think it a privilege to have sex with them and to mother their children. They were taught that it was like having a relationship with God. False doctrine is indeed a slippery slope.

By their very nature, apostates are subtle and clandestine in their approach. They pretend loyalty to Christ while actively undermining the truth of the Gospel, that their lies will be willingly accepted by gullible listeners. "Do not judge according to appearance, but judge with righteous judgment." (John 7:24) Many have read that verse and taught that we should not be judgmental. That is the complete opposite of what it means. It means we don't judge by appearance but according to Scripture. Gullibility can be disobedience to the Word of God. Becoming overzealous in becoming a critic can lead to developing a critical spirit, which is entirely different. We DON'T need more critical people on a witch hunt; we DO need more people who are capable of critically analyzing and discerning teachers and their teaching.

The Bible teaches that a person with a quarrelsome nature is unfit for spiritual leadership. "A servant of the Lord must not quarrel but be gentle to all." (2 Timothy 2:24) But there are some things worth fighting for and nothing surpasses the purity of the Gospel. While contending for the faith, we must never become apathetic to the proposition that there is a battle to be waged for truth. Apathy may be the most dangerous enemy facing the church today. Subtleties, lies and deceptions in the name of God only make it more difficult to discern the true from the false.

Jude, in his brief epistle, presented three ways to identify an apostate. First, by "their character." "Ungodly" is one of the key words in the epistle of Jude. In verse 15 alone, he uses the word four times. Ungodly means they would not retain the things of God in their minds or hearts, much less teach them. They are devoid of anything that resembles true Christian character. They have no integrity, nor do they demonstrate the fruit of godliness.

Second, by "their conduct." These "ungodly men" would be engaged in activities that would make the devil blush. "The works of the flesh are evident...adultery, fornication, uncleanness, lewdness, idolatry, sorcery, hatred, contentions, jealousies, outbursts of wrath, selfish ambitions, dissensions, heresies, envy, murders, drunkenness, revelries and the like." (Galatians 5:19-21) Notice the first four have to do with moral impurity. That is not a coincidence. Without sound doctrine, there will always be a moral vacuum. Wrong will win out over right when the truth of Scripture and the Spirit of God are absent.

"The new postmodern church is easy to embrace," stated one secular writer in describing it. "Because it doesn't demonize youth culture, Marilyn Manson, South Park or gangster rap like traditional fundamentalists." When I was growing up, our generation of young preachers were taught the church should impact the world. Now we are taught the world should impact the church.

Third, by their creed. Apostates "deny the only Lord God and our Lord Jesus Christ." This one fact is at the heart of every false teaching found in any false teacher's "doctrine". Why? Because it is the foundational, watershed truth of the Christian faith. Today, some leaders have openly and publicly denied the deity of Christ and remained as respected leaders in their denominations, even retaining the title of bishop. The root problem with all false teachers is the deity of Christ. They are rebels with a cause, fulfilling their lusts and filling their coffers with the gold of gullible followers. They may profess "Lord, Lord," but they do not do what He says (Luke 6:46). In Paul's letter to Titus, he states, "They profess to know God, but in works they deny Him, being abominable, disobedient and disqualified for every good work." (Titus 1:16) That belief precedes behavior was never more accurate. Their creed determines their conduct, which is detestable.

Many in the evangelical movement have been kidnapped by postmodern thought that has transformed certainty into doubt. In fact, if a writer or speaker questions the validity of a Biblical position, rather than being reproached, he is held up as a hero, while the one who demands allegiance to the Bible is held up as "arrogant". This approach has been called by some a "hermeneutic of humility". It is neither good hermeneutics nor humility. It is arrogance in extreme masquerading as piety (it says God didn't REALLY mean what He said, and IF He said it, we can't be sure WHAT He meant). That violates the first rule of interpretation, which is: Always be true to the author. If we can't know what the author (God) is saying, how can He hold us accountable for our sins? We may be wrong on what sin is. It all depends on what "is" is. Sound familiar?

If we weave that postmodern thread to its logical conclusion, no one can be certain about anything. Without a spiritual compass (the Bible), every man can be "right in his own eyes," and there are no eternal absolutes.

Others would give lip service to the Lordship of Christ but refuse to submit to His authority in matters of conduct. We have replaced confession and repentance with "recovery" programs that bypass uncomfortable words like "confess". Often professional therapists replace preachers of the Word that once brought conviction and produced regenerated saints.

So how do we survive this morass of moral mud? In the midst of this onslaught of postmodern sensibilities, Scripture is clear. We are to stand in the gap, contend for the faith and remain faithful to the end. The enemies of the cross have always levied their heaviest artillery against the preaching of the cross, its teaching of substitutionary atonement, and the deity of Jesus. One author referred to the substitutionary atonement as "twisted", "morally dubious" and "a form of cosmic child abuse." VARIOUS EMERGING CHURCHES AND WEBSITES HAVE REPEATEDLY CALLED FOR A WHOLESALE DISMANTLING OF THE VERY DOCTRINES THAT EVANGELICALS HAVE HISTORICALLY HELD AS THE ANCHOR FOR THEIR VERY SOUL.

While the attacks came from the outside church walls from atheists and infidels, the church withstood the onslaught. But now, as the battle has been joined by interlopers, who look and talk like we do, the issues have become more and more confusing. It is time that we who believe the Word of God reclaim our spiritual heritage and demand that the lines of orthodoxy—once clearly recognized—be reestablished.

Many see a parallel between the political and religious landscape of the postmodern era. Both have had clearly defined battlegrounds and issues. Now the issues are muddied and the lines are nearly unrecognizable. Saboteurs have crept in and stolen the clarity of the Bible. Many are confused as to who is the real prophet and who is the false prophet. Spiritual terrorists play havoc with spiritual values and teaching as terrorists play havoc with the general population.

Western society, by and large, does not have the spiritual backbone to stand up to the danger of apostasy. We would rather have "peace at any price". But abandon moral values, lose your spiritual compass and put a little spiritual terrorism into the mix, and things change in a hurry. The climate now is open for any and all belief systems to be introduced into the vacuum.

Jude reminded us to "remember what was prophesied." If we fail to learn from the past, we are destined to repeat it. We have been warned by the Bible, history and experience. We have no excuse for allowing the apostatizing of the truth.

As we are warned to remember, we are also reminded to remain faithful, "building yourselves up in your most Holy faith." Be encouraging each other. Be strengthened, become mature. Jude exhorts us to reach out. The people in the pew who need the truth of the Word of God are dependent on we who believe the Bible to declare it with power and clarity. We must not only oppose false teachers but rescue those who have been captured by their false doctrines.

Fight the good fight. Stay in the battle. Unity in the Church must be sought with all our heart. But there is one battle that is worth fighting; one cause worth dying for, and this is it. Fighting error spawned in Hell does not mean we have to battle each other.

Chapter 6

The Contemporary Music Wars

For many years, the battle has raged around the issue of traditional music versus the ever-increasingly popular new contemporary praise and worship music. Often it is called "the worship wars." Think of that. How inconceivable—those two words back-to-back. Saying "worship wars" is like saying dry water or cold heat. The two are mutually exclusive. A few years ago, God gave me a message that has been used in many churches to bring a truce in the "worship wars." If you are experiencing the same struggle in your church, I pray God will particularly use these words for you. If you haven't experienced the battle, you may well do so in the future. I want to say three things that are critical. I ask for an open mind and heart as you consider them.

FIRST OF ALL, I WANT TO ASK THE YOUNGER PEOPLE TO RESPECTFULLY UNDERSTAND WHY THE OLD MUSIC IS SO IMPORTANT TO OLDER PEOPLE. THERE ARE MANY REASONS. I SUGGEST FIVE.

1. The old music has a dignity that older people feel is worthy of God. It's never quite been said like, "When morning gilds the skies, my heart awakening cries: May Jesus Christ be praised" or "A mighty fortress is our God, a bulwark never failing." This grand and glorious music is, in the heart and mind of senior adults, consistent with the majesty and dignity of the God whom they have revered and worshipped since childhood.

2. The old music emotionally ties those of us who are older to another time when things were better. What an unstable, frightening world we live in! In my city only one in ten dwelling places is inhabited by a traditional nuclear family where one man is married to one woman, who live with their own set of children. Nine out of ten are inhabited by homosexuals, divorcees, live-ins, singles, blended families, etc. That is not to say that being single is a shame. It is to say that everything that is nailed down is coming up. There was stability and security in the past, and the older we get, the harder change becomes. That great old music ties us to another time when things were more stable. It is music we grew up on. We sang the great Christmas carols at Christmastime and "Power of the Blood," "Just as I Am" and "Saved, Saved, Saved" during revivals. We like things like they've always been. Move the furniture, change the bed, scoot the dresser to another side of the room; that's hard for senior adults. Changing cars is hard. Changing towns, cities or churches is hard. Changing jobs is most difficult. And nothing reigns in our hearts like the music of our faith. It is the spiritual heartbeat, the soul of who we are as believers. Our music is everything to us. That's how we remember. That's how we express emotion. That's how we make it through the day. And to think of a world in which it is fast slipping away is extremely difficult for the senior adult.

3. It ministered to us in times of great need. As I stood by Mother's grave, they sang "In the Garden" and "Sweet By and By." The night my sister was converted, they were singing, "Pass Me Not Oh Gentle Savior." When I was discouraged, I often remembered the words to "I'd Rather Have Jesus" and "Leaning on the Everlasting Arms." These songs are important to me. These songs are meaningful. They are important to the spiritual and emotional stability and security of the senior adults because they ministered to us in the past, and they desperately and earnestly long not to lose them. They will need them today, and they will need them again tomorrow.

Some time ago, a Navy veteran told me, "Pastor, the new music is okay, and I'll never criticize it, but let me tell you why the old songs are so important to me. I was on a ship with 3,000 other sailors in World War II. I truly believe I was the only Christian there. Living for the Lord was difficult. There was no help, no support. Many evenings I would go to the back of the ship and sit for an hour or two watching the sunset, watching the waves as they separated behind the ship, and sing those old songs. Had I not had 'The Old Rugged Cross,' 'Jesus Keep Me Near the Cross,' 'What a Friend We Have in Jesus' and 'Amazing Grace' to sing, I don't know if I could have made it. They were my very survival."

4. Many of us learned our theology from those songs. I grew up on topical sermons. My pastor always preached topical series. Seldom, if ever, did I hear a series through the Bible, verse by verse, from an Old Testament or New Testament book. So we learned much of our theology from those great hymns. Songs of redemption and security. Songs of salvation and comfort. Songs of Lordship and Holiness. Sing the five verses aloud of "One Day." Those five verses contain virtually the entire New Testament story in a nutshell. Those who are older find it difficult to leave behind that which meant so much to them in their early and mid-year spiritual development.

5. Older people love the old music because of the desire to leave a legacy. I am beyond 70 years of age, and increasingly I am impelled to think about my children and grandchildren and the world we shall leave them. It is not a pretty world. It is not a secure world. Is there not much we can pass on to them to make their survival a bit more certain in a world that is fast becoming more and more uncertain? Everything in my heart wants to leave a legacy. I want my children to know the joys I have known, the power of a great family, the blessing of friendship, the joy of integrity and the peace of God. And much of that revolves around the music of my life. Frankly, I cannot conceive of a world in which my children never heard of "The Old Rugged Cross," "Love Lifted Me," "Down at the Cross" or "Since Jesus Came into My Heart." But I'm afraid that's the kind of world we're going to have in 10 or 20 years.

So to those who are younger—young people, young adults, young pastors—we love you and appreciate you so much. You are the hope; you are the future; you are today; you are tomorrow; you are everything. But please understand why we hunger so for a place of honor and respect for the music that means so much to us. And frankly, I think we owe something to our senior adults. They have paid the bills, they have built the church, they've perpetuated the faith, they've been faithful; and we are here because they were here. If you do not have a service where you at least blend the music and allow the great hymns to be sung along with the new contemporary music, then consider starting a second service; one with only traditional music for the older people who love it so much.

NOW I WANT TO HELP THOSE OF YOU WHO ARE OLDER TO UNDERSTAND WHY THE NEW MUSIC IS SO IMPORTANT TO THE YOUNG. And I must tell you straight up, that unless you can grasp this and find a way to include, or even prioritize, this kind of new music, your congregation will get more and more grey, and in 20 or 30 years, you will have no congregation at all. You fight the new music; you reject it at your own peril. It's here to stay, and if you cannot find a way to honor it and use it as well as the older music, you will not reach the young. The fact is that only one-third of Southern Baptist churches baptized even six or more teenagers last year. One-third baptized only two to five teenagers, and one-third baptized none. We are losing the battle. We have a perishing generation, and unless something drastic happens there's going to be no tomorrow for us. We must reach the youth, and the music is their life. If we do not understand that, we will fail as missionaries to a very needy generation.

Let me help those of you who are older to understand why the new music is so important to the young.

1. The new music is TO Jesus, not ABOUT Jesus. Get hold of that. It is *to* Jesus, not just *about* Jesus. Search the pages of your hymnal, and you will find that probably no more than five percent of the hymns and Gospel songs are addressed *to* the Lord Jesus Christ. They are testimonies telling me and telling others *about* Jesus. They do not address Him and personally worship and connect with Him. Why is this absolutely critical? To answer this you must understand what's happening in our world.

There are three basic tenets in society: the home, the church and the government. In the home, we have a 60% divorce rate. As stated, 90% of our residences are not inhabited by traditional families. Young people are quickly losing confidence in the home, because most of them have never really seen a real home and family, let alone a Christian home and family. The second tenet of society is the government. This young generation has lived through two decades and more of political corruption. Congressmen send homosexual emails to congressional pages. While Newt Gingridge was leading the impeachment effort against Bill Clinton in the Monica Lewinsky affair, he now acknowledges he himself was having an affair. Many of us remember Gary Hart; Watergate; Richard Nixon; sad and sordid stories about John Kennedy; not to mention Ted Kennedy and the apparent cover-up at Chapaquidic.

In the church, scandal after scandal arises. Virtually every week, I hear a new one. Recently two of the most prominent ministers in Colorado acknowledged that they were having homosexual relationships with other men. 50% of ministers say they would quit the ministry if they had the opportunity to take another job. 1500 ministers of all denominations quit the ministry every month. Over 50% of pastors acknowledge seeking out pornography on the internet. Jim Bakker, Jimmy Swaggart—on and on goes the list. And our young society looks at the church in the same category as the government and the home and says there's nothing to it. And so they are tremendously unstable; searching, seeking; their feet in the wet concrete of an undependable, unstable and unbelievable society. They have rejected the society; they have rejected its basic tenets. They have rejected tradition. They have largely rejected denominationalism and structure and organization. They seem not to care about anything.

But the good news is that they still hunger for Jesus Christ. He is still the true Light that lights every man that comes into the world. The problem is they don't know that Jesus is what they hunger for, so they try to fill the empty spot with drugs, sexual immorality and a thousand other things. But every once in a while, when a young person gets tuned on to Jesus, their level of commitment is through the roof. They're easily won to Christ. They're not anti-Jesus. Many are simply anti-establishment for the reasons listed above. And when they find Jesus, they are passionate about Him. They have found the only stable, secure, dependable thing they have ever known, and it's more important than anything—as it should be. And so for them to praise Jesus, to love Jesus, to talk to Jesus, to sing to Jesus, to worship Jesus in music is everything. They don't want to talk *about* Jesus; they don't want to sing *about* Jesus. They want to talk *to*

Jesus; they want to sing *to* Jesus. Examine the words of the contemporary praise music of the day. You may be surprised to find it is not *about* Jesus, it is primarily *to* Jesus. It addresses Him, it hooks into Him, and it is everything to the young. Because of the instability and unreality of the society in which they live, when they find Jesus they are passionate about it and their love affair with Him scintillates in its expression through their music.

Have you noticed that in many churches, the pastor doesn't even sit on the platform? There are no choirs and virtually no special music. This young generation doesn't care about hymnals; they don't care about how we look on the platform. They don't care about being sung to by the choir or a soloist. They don't care about bulletins and orders of service. They just care about Jesus. And how can we fault that? The new music is *to* Jesus and not *about* Jesus and we must understand that, rejoice in that and not discredit it.

2. The new music is music they understand. Their whole world is music. If you're going to communicate with young people today, you're going to have to speak their language — and their language is music. Jam boxes and earphones, CDs, iPods, iPhones, U Tube, My Space, cell phones, downloads; it's basically all about music. Music is their world, it sets their standards, it determines their priorities, it influences their lives, it sets their moral pattern and influences their convictions. It is everything. If you're going to go to Germany as a missionary, you will have to learn to speak German. You don't make the people of Germany learn to speak English. If you're going to go to Nigeria as a missionary, you'll have to learn to speak Ebo, Swahili, Uraba or Housa. Those are the languages they speak. You must speak to them in their language. You will not force them to learn your language in order to hear you. They will simply walk away.

A few years ago Time Magazine said there were 37 million young people in America between the ages of 14 and 24, and 35 million of them had never been to church and weren't going. They said their whole world is music, and added: if a teenager today has $15.00 and is dying of hunger, he would spend his last $15.00 to buy the latest rock CD before he would buy a sandwich, and simply starve to death. It is their language. They're not speaking our language. And we're going to have to put our message in their language to reach them, to communicate the Gospel to them. One-half of 1% of all music sold in music stores is classical music. It's good to try to raise the level of music appreciation, but if we don't start raising the level of interest by communicating to this young generation in the language they speak, we are going to get nowhere.

When John and Charles Wesley were converted, they hungered to get the Gospel in to the mind and heart of the secular world to which they were called. In order to do so, as musicians and preachers, they went to the bars and taverns and listened to the kind of music that was being sung. They took the tunes, learned the melodies and simply wrote Gospel words to them. That is exactly what many young musical missionaries are doing today. Whether it is hard rock, soft rock, or in between rock, the music is still the medium for the young people today through which we must preach the unchanging Gospel of Jesus Christ. Please keep in mind, that we absolutely must never compromise the purity of the Gospel. The message must never change, but the methods must be ever changing.

3. The new music is primarily Scripture set to music. And how can we fault that? Again, search your Hymnal. Barely five percent of the Hymns are nothing but Scripture set to music. In the new contemporary music barely five percent are not!

4. Things Change. Things Grow. The Apostle Paul speaks of at least three kinds of music: psalms, hymns and spiritual songs. Apparently there has always been an evolution of types of music being introduced throughout the history of the Judeo-Christian faith. Perhaps Paul had something like that in mind when he said, "I have become all things to all men; that I might by all means win some." The MESSAGE must NEVER change, but the METHODS and means must be EVER changing to bring an ever-changing generation to THE KNOWLEDGE OF the truth.

Have you ever wondered why God saw to the preservation of the words of the oldest music of the Judeo-Christian faith in the Psalms? The hymnbook of the Old Testament is preserved for us in our Bible. But, why did He not see to the preservation of the music? We don't know how the 23rd Psalm went. We cannot identify the melody of Psalm 51 or Psalm 91. Why did God preserve the words but not the music? I think it is because He knew EVERY GENERATION

WOULD WRITE ITS OWN MUSIC. Remember, there's nothing sacred about guitars or organs, bongo drums or violins, robes or blue jeans, fast or slow, loud or soft, E-flat or C-major. Music is amoral. Music is only a means by which we express our hearts and feelings. Please use the new music to express the old Gospel to the hearts of a dying generation. It is my strong conviction that if you do not do so, you will be a part of the problem rather than the solution in losing an entire generation.

Yes, things do change. If they didn't, you'd probably be singing Gregorian chants today. That's what we used to do, you know. Then came hymns; now comes contemporary music; tomorrow, perhaps something else. When I began in full time Christian ministry, I was an evangelist. When we went to town for an old-fashioned revival, we would simply print out a few dozen handbills, get a roll of scotch tape and go to the grocery stores, service stations and drive-ins and put them in the window. Today if you are going to advertise your campaign, you better get on the internet. One of my students said recently, "If I want to communicate with my teenagers, I must use the internet. They will not answer a call, a letter, a card, or respond to a pamphlet about an event. I must use the internet; it is their language." And so is music.

Let's review. I have asked the younger people to understand why the old music is so important to those of us who are older. I have asked the older people to understand why the new music is so important to the young.

Now, I WANT YOU BOTH TO UNDERSTAND WHY NEITHER IS IMPORTANT TO GOD. Think about that a minute. Just pause and reflect. Do you think God really cares whether music is fast or slow, loud or soft? In John 4, Jesus said something that ought forever to put an end to the battle. When the Samaritan woman met Jesus at the well, she engaged Him in spiritual conversation. After He was getting too close, talking about the several husbands she had had and the man with whom she was now living, she quickly changed the subject and abruptly asked the Lord, "Sir, you Jews say that we are to worship in Jerusalem. We Samaritans say one ought to worship here on Mount Gerizim" (the place where they were standing). "Let's talk about where one ought to worship."

Jesus' answer was wonderful. He said to her, "Woman, believe Me, the hour is coming when neither on this mountain nor in Jerusalem will you worship the Father. You worship what you do not know. We know what we worship, for salvation is of the Jews. But the hour is coming, and now is, when the true worshippers will worship the Father in Spirit and truth. For the Father seeks such to worship Him." "God is a Spirit, and those who worship Him must worship Him in Spirit and truth." Jesus refused to acknowledge the superiority of Samaritan worship on Mount Gerizim or Jewish worship in Jerusalem. He cut straight to the chase, and said "Woman, that is not the important issue. All that matters is one thing: that you worship God in Spirit and in truth." All the accoutrements of Jewish and Samaritan worship are irrelevant, nonessential and totally unimportant. What does matter, however, is the way you worship in your heart.

He told us two things alone were essential to acceptable worship. First it must be in spirit. That simply means it must be sincere, from your heart. Secondly, it must be in truth, based on the Word of God. My dear reader, if one is worshipping Jesus Christ, in accordance with the Word of God and doing so with all their heart, it doesn't matter whether he's dancing a jig or sitting in a cathedral—God is honored, God is blessed, and God approves his worship. The devil has us running in circles over the issue of how to worship, when the answer is clearly stated in John 4. It doesn't matter about the physical accoutrements of worship; all that matters is that it be sincere and Biblical.

Let me ask you a question. Here is a group of young people sitting in their shorts singing songs around a campfire at Youth Camp. Over here, a Southern Gospel church singing Stamps Baxter music, barreling out, "I'll Fly Away" from a songbook with shaped notes. Over here is a church in Africa, where scantily clad Africans are chanting and dancing around their hut. Here is a great cathedral in London, with a 5-million dollar organ, seven-fold amen, and robed choir. Do you really think God cares? And by the way, WHAT ARE YOU GOING TO DO IF YOU GET TO HEAVEN AND FIND OUT GOD LIKES RAP?

The Samaritan religion was quite different from Judaism. The Samaritans were half Jew and half Gentile. They had nothing to do with the Jews, and the Jews had nothing to do with them. Their worship, their religion; everywhere there were differences. Here are just a few.

The Jews worshipped in the temple in Jerusalem. The Samaritans' temple was on Mount Gerizim. The Jews believe they descended from Abraham. The Samaritans, that they were converts of a lion. The Jewish alter was quite small. The Samaritan altar of worship was quite elaborate—65 x 65 feet with great pillars and statues. In Jewish worship, the Gentiles worshipped in the outer court. In Samaritan worship, they sat together. The Jews were city people; the Samaritans were country people. The Jews believed Gerizim was cursed; the Samaritans believed Jerusalem was cursed. Sounds like the debate between the new music and the old today, doesn't it? The Jews accepted the entire Old Testament. The Samaritans; only the Pentateuch. The Jews believed the Messiah would come through Judah. The Samaritans, that He would come through Joseph. The Jews described God in anthropomorphic terms. The Samaritans would never do so. The Jews were liberal in their interpretation of the civil law. The Samaritans were very strict. The Jews would not use God's name, Yahweh. The Samaritans did. The Jews believed in dialogue with Islam. The Samaritans did not.

But nowhere was the difference greater than in the manner in which they worshipped. Jewish worship was very simple. Samaritan worship was elaborate, loud, and over-the-edge. The Jews sang straight ahead, side by side. In Samaritan worship, two groups called rightists and leftists faced each other and sang antiphonally. The Jews adlibbed syllables in singing. In Samaritan worship, there was no adlibbing; the melody was structured and strict. The Jews sang one text only to one melody. The Samaritans sang the same text to many different varieties of melodies.

L. A. Bernstein, world-noted authority on the Samaritan religion, states that the most obvious difference in the two forms of worship was the firm commitment to their musical traditions of the Samaritans. They would not flux; they would not bend; they would not adapt. Dr. Bernstein pointed out that in Jesus' day, there were approximately 1,200,000 persons in the world practicing Samaritan worship. Today, there are about 600. One must wonder if there is any connection to those statistics and their refusal to change.

In my city of Houston, Texas, new mosques are opened all the time. And other religions are growing. Young people are being drawn into the occult, attempting suicide, hooked on drugs, dying of aids and getting all their values from their computer and their music. Let me ask you a question. Will you be willing to die to reach your grandkids for Jesus Christ? I know you would. Now another question: Would you be willing to change your music for them in order to see them come to Christ? Imagine your church, 20 years from now, at the rate you are going. Because this I can tell you, if you are not finding a way to embrace the new music, either in blended services or two alternative services offering a choice of both kinds of music, your church is getting older and grayer. And one day, it may be gone.

We face two challenges. The first is to not throw out the old music. It's great music; it's important; it meant much to us. And we need to honor it and embrace it. Secondly, we need to find ways to incorporate the new music. Again, either two services or blended services are the only answers I have found. But you must do both; we must understand each other and we must remember: God says the only kind of worship that is important to Him is that which comes from a heart of loving sincerity and Biblical fidelity.

I spent six years discussing, analyzing, considering, talking and preparing to go to an additional service in our church that was fully contemporary. The First Baptist Church in Houston is nearly 170 years old. It is the second oldest Baptist church in Texas, second only to First Baptist Church of Independence. Things don't change easily in a church like ours. Finally I realized two things. First, I would have opposition; not everyone would support me. But two, I *had* to begin a contemporary service. With fear and trepidation, yet confidence in the peace and leadership of the Holy Spirit, we began that service. We prepared for 200 persons. The first service had 900! By the time I left, there were 2500. Today there are hundreds, even thousands more than that, as our young pastor Gregg Matte continues to provide both kinds of music for both kinds of folks.

Before I finally bit the bullet and began the new contemporary service, I called a Sunday school rally for all of our 50-year old and above members. Hundreds were there, even thousands. I spent an hour explaining to them why we were going to that new service. I asked the question, "How many of you have kids or their kids that don't go to church, don't love the Lord, are not Christians, and it's breaking your heart?" Over half the congregation raised their hands. Then I said to them, "When you walk down the hallway to your class next Sunday morning and you hear music coming out of the auditorium that you don't like, remember this: it's not for you, it's for your kids and grandkids."

Chapter 7

Calvinism

S imply stated, the theology of Calvinism is basically true. The problem is, however, the opposite is also true. What we have here is a mystery; an irreconcilable mystery. And you might as well ask Einstein to teach the Theory of Relativity to your dog as to try to explain this to the human mind. The Bible speaks of mysteries. There are many things we cannot reconcile and do not know. I have found that once you take any side of a mystery and press it to its extremity without considering the counterbalance doctrine, you usually end up in heresy. Jesus is divine; He is also human. The deity of Jesus and the humanity of Jesus cannot be reconciled. They must simply be accepted and affirmed. Take the deity of Jesus to its extreme and ignore His humanity and you have Gnosticism. A savior who is simply an aberration of the mind, a phantom, a ghost who had no physical body, because all matter is evil and He could, therefore, not have had a body. This heresy leads us to the position of a cross with no blood and a world with no Savior. If you take the doctrine of His humanity to the extreme and ignore His deity, you have humanism and outright liberalism. Which is true? Is He human or divine? The answer to that question is simply: YES. Understand it, no. Believe it, you'd better.

In many ways, the same is true of the theology of Calvinism. Let's look together at the five basic points of Calvinism, often called

T.U.L.I.P. As we consider these thoughts, I shall be quoting generously from a booklet by Dr. Curtis Hutson.

1. Total Inability. The doctrine of Total Inability simply means that unless God overpowers a man and gives him that ability, he will never come to Christ. The Bible does speak of Total Depravity, which simply means there is nothing good in man to earn his salvation or to deserve it. But the Bible never teaches that people are lost because they have no ability to come to Christ. Jesus said in John 5:40, "You will not come to me, that you might have life." Notice, He did not say you CANNOT come; rather you WILL NOT come. Jesus wept over Jerusalem and said, "Oh Jerusalem, Jerusalem... how often would I have gathered thy children together even as a hen gathers her chicks under her wings, but you would not." Notice again, he did not say you *could not*, he said you *would not*. The issue is not a matter of ability, rather a matter of the stubbornness and hard-heartedness of their unbelief. In Revelations 22:17 Jesus says, "Whosoever will, may come unto Me." In John 5:40, He says, "You will not come unto me." It is clearly the will of man here in view. He did not say you *cannot* come, but you *will not* come.

There are three capacities which give us human personhood and set us above the animal kingdom: knowledge, emotion and will. Animals have knowledge; they know things. Animals have emotion; they feel things. But they have no will, no volition and no capacity to make moral judgments. They are not free moral agents. They cannot make decisions for or against God. But we do. We have a will. We have the capacity to choose morally and spiritually. So it is that which sets us above the animal kingdom and makes us in the image of God. The will is particularly sacred to God, and He will never force it. He will never coerce our will.

This is a mystery, and we shall never fully comprehend all mysteries until we know as we are known, when we see Him as He is and shall be like Him. Until then, we simply have to give God credit for knowing some things we do not know. If I ask you to raise your hand, and you raised your hand, why did you do so? Because I asked you? Yes, but also because you chose to. You would not have just raised it had I not asked you, and you did not have to raise it if you did not choose to. So both your will and my sovereignty went into the raising of your hand. Both had to happen. If one or the other had not happened, your hand would not have gone up. The same is true with Biblical mysteries. Both things are true. There are many counterbalance doctrines in Scripture which again must be harmonized and reconciled, though not totally understandable, or heresy develops. If you throw a baseball to me and I hit it with a bat, does the bat hit the ball or does the ball hit the bat? Both. May God help us to keep in focus the importance of balance as we consider these pages.

2. Unconditional Election. That is, God chooses us and the individual has absolutely nothing to do with it. In Calvin's book of "INSTITUTES," Book Three, Chapter 23, he writes, "Not all men are created with similar destinies, but eternal life is foreordained for some; eternal damnation for others." Let me ask you a question. Can there be any doubt whatsoever that the doctrine of Calvinism lessens the evangelistic and missionary fervor of the believer? Question number two: WHO'S BEHIND THAT? God certainly *does* select individuals for *special service*. He chose Abraham and Isaac. He chose Paul and Peter to be His special instruments, just as He chose Israel to be the human instrumentality through which He would give us the law, the prophets, the ceremonies and ultimately he Gospel and the Lord Jesus Himself. He had to choose some entity through which to come. He chose the Jewish people. Often, Ephesians 1:4 is chosen as a proof of election without any capacity or input of man to choose to receive God's choice of him. It says, "He has chosen us in Him, before the foundation of the world." But notice, as Dr. Hutson so well points out, that's only half the verse. The full verse reads, "According as He hath chosen us in Him before the foundation of the world, THAT WE SHOULD BE HOLY AND WITHOUT BLAME BEFORE HIM IN LOVE." This verse says nothing about being chosen for Heaven and Hell, but chosen that we should be holy and without blame as believers. John 15:16 is often only quoted in part: "You have not chosen Me, but I have chosen you." Again, however, the entire verse reads, "You have not chosen Me, but I have chosen you and ordained you that you should go forth and bear fruit...." Chosen for salvation is not in view here. Chosen for fruitfulness for every believer certainly is.

2 Peter 3:9 says, "He is not willing that any should perish, but that all should come to the knowledge of the truth." It is God's will that all be saved. 1 Timothy 2:4 says, "Who will have all men to be saved and come to the knowledge of the truth." God's will is for all men to be saved, but God has given man a will as well. God's will is not always done. It was not God's will for man to fall in the garden. But when man sinned, God moved in to provide salvation for all who would believe. It is not God's will for men to get drunk, commit adultery and murder each other. But still they do. We live in a fallen world. Human depravity has a will and it often exercises that will against God. Take the free will from man, and you reduce him to a dog. Does God predestinate some to be saved and others to go to Hell, so that they have no free choice in the matter? Absolutely not! John 3:36, "He that believeth on the Son hath everlasting life, and he that believeth not the Son shall not see light, but the wrath of God abideth on him." How could anything be more plain?

3. Limited Atonement. By Limited Atonement, Calvin meant that Christ died only for the elect, for those He planned and ordained to go to Heaven. He did not die for those He planned and ordained to go to Hell. Such a position contradicts many plain Scriptures. 1 John 2:2 says, "He is the propitiation for our sins, and not for ours only, but also for the sins of THE WHOLE WORLD." 1 Timothy 2:5-6 says, "The man Christ Jesus; who gave Himself a ransom FOR ALL." John 4:42 says, "Now we believe, not because by seeing, but we have heard Him ourselves, and know that He is indeed the Christ, the Savior of THE WORLD." John 4:14 says, "And we have seen and do testify that the Father sent the Son to be the Savior of THE WORLD." John 3:17, "For God sent not his son into the world to condemn the world, but that THE WORLD might through Him be saved."

If Jesus did not die for the sins of the whole world, then John 3:16 is only a cruel joke played on the human race. Isaiah 53:6 says, "All we like sheep have gone astray, we have turned everyone to his own way, and the Lord hath laid on Him the iniquity of us all." There are two ALLs in this verse. The first ALL speaks of the universal fact of sin—"ALL we, like sheep, have gone astray." And the second ALL speaks of universal atonement—"And the Lord hath laid on

Him the iniquity of us ALL." The ALL in the first part of Isaiah 53:6 covers the same group as the ALL of the last part of Isaiah 53:6. If ALL went astray, the iniquities of ALL were laid on Christ. His death was for every man. Hebrews 2:9 says, "But we see Jesus, who was made a little lower than the angels, for the suffering of death, crowned with glory and honour; that He by the grace of God should taste death for EVERY MAN." 1 Timothy 2:5-6 says, "For there is one God and one mediator between God and man, the man Christ Jesus, who gave Himself a ransom for ALL." Romans 8:32 says, "He spared not His own Son, but delivered Him up for us ALL; how shall He not with Him also freely give us all things." Atonement is not limited; it is as universal as sin. Romans 5:20 says, "But where sin abounded, grace did much more abound."

4. Irresistible Grace. Boiled down to its ultimate simplicity, this simply means God can and does force His grace upon us—a doctrine which is totally in contradiction with the rest of the Word of God where our Lord gave man a free will and made us free moral agents created above the animal kingdom. In fact, there is no such thing as irresistible grace. Nowhere in the Bible does the word IRRESISTIBLE appear before the word GRACE. If Calvin had talked about the irresistible drawing power of God, it would have made more sense. Rather, he represents grace as an irresistible act of God impelling man to be saved who has no choice in the matter, and forcing upon him what he actually may not want and over which he has no control at all. Thusly, we are simply animals, robots or statues—not humans made in the image of God. As creatures made in God's image, if God has a heart, we have a heart. If God has a mind, we have a mind. If God makes choices, we make choices. If God has a will, we have a will. The Bible says nothing of irresistible grace. To the contrary, Proverbs 29:1 says, "He that being often reproved, hardeneth his heart, shall suddenly be cut off; and that without remedy." Notice the word "often." It is a constantly repeated action in which man continually hardens his heart. In Matthew 12, Jesus told the Pharisees they had hardened their hearts so often, resisted the Holy Spirit so long, that they were beyond salvation— they had actually committed the unpardonable sin. In Acts 7:51, Stephen said, "Ye stiff-necked and uncircumcised in heart and ears, you do always resist the Holy Ghost; as your fathers did, so do you." Calvin says you cannot resist the Holy Spirit. The Bible says men can and did and do. Whom shall we believe?

5. Perseverance of the Saints. Unquestionably, the Bible speaks of the eternal security of the believer. We are complete in him. We are washed with the blood, saved by the cross, born again of the Spirit and sealed by Him unto everlasting life. By the way, how long does everlasting last? One would think forever, does it not? The Bible teaches nothing about the saints persevering. It does, however, teach that the saints are *preserved*, and that is greatly different. Perseverance is one thing, preservation quite another. The saints do indeed not persevere, hang in there, faithful; they are preserved. Matthew 24:13 says, "He that shall endure to the end shall be saved." He is simply saying that the saved shall endure to the end. It is the nature of saving faith that it endures.

Both James and 1 John were written to say if you're profession of faith was real, if you truly have salvation, you can test your life to know that it is genuine by whether or not it is bearing fruit. It is the nature of hypocrisy that it professes salvation, talks a good game, dies and goes to Hell. Not because it lost salvation, but because it never had it in the first place. It is, however, the nature of saving faith that it endures; it lasts; it sticks.

It is not the lasting that makes salvation real. It is lasting which validates and authenticates the fact that it IS real. Salvation is real; salvation is eternal. But it is not because we endure; it is because the Father preserves us and works His grace in and through us. Jude 1 says, "Jude, the servant of Jesus Christ, and brother of James; to them that are sanctified by God the Father and PRESERVED in Jesus Christ." 1 Thessalonians 5:23 says, "And the very God of peace, sanctify you wholly; and I pray God your whole spirit and soul and body be PRESERVED, blameless unto the coming of our Lord." In 1 Peter 1:4-5, He says, "Through an inheritance, incorruptible and undefiled, and that fadeth not away, RESERVED in Heaven for you who are KEPT by the power of God through faith unto salvation, ready to be revealed at the last time." In John 10:27-29, Jesus said, "My sheep hear My voice, and I know them and they follow me. And I will give unto them eternal life, and they shall never perish. Neither shall any man pluck them out of My hand. My Father which gave them to Me is greater than all, and no man is able to pluck them out of My Father's hand." Does that sound like the perseverance of the saints, or the preservation of the Father? I do not believe in the perseverance of the saints. I believe in the preservation of the Savior. To be sure, the Bible teaches the eternal security of the believer, but we are secure because we are KEPT BY God, not that we keep ourselves IN God. We are held in His hand. Ephesians 4:30 reminds us, "We have been sealed by the Holy Spirit until the day of redemption."

Chapter 8

Preaching to Today's People

S ociety has changed, and in many ways preaching needs to change. Not the message; that is eternal, it never changes. Youth for Christ used to have a slogan, "Geared to the times but anchored to the Rock." That's good. God's perfect, inerrant, infallible Word is what Southern Baptists fought and bled for and is the truth.

A baseball is a baseball. It is a 2-3/8 inch sphere, which is thrown from pitching mounds 60 ft, 6 inches to home plate from the bush leagues to Yankee Stadium. The baseball never changes, but the way it is pitched determines the effectiveness of both losers and winners. Please keep clearly in focus the priority of what I am saying. Under no circumstances can the purity of the inerrant Word of God, the Gospel of Jesus Christ—salvation only by Him—be compromised in anything we preach or teach. It is the only eternal, endless, ageless, authoritative, effective message we have, and pity the man who dilutes it, waters it down or substitutes anything else for it. We're talking primarily about delivery, and that is more important than you may ever realize. The baseball is the same from the minors to the majors. But the way it's delivered determines the champions.

Let's talk about preaching to today's people.

1. Don't get too cute with the outline. I listen to a lot of preachers and go away with the feeling they wanted me to be more impressed with their outline than their content. Frankly, in my opinion, most preaching done in Southern Baptist pulpits today makes the outline far too prominent. The outline is not the thing. It is only the framework on which we hang the truth. Let me raise the question: Is the purpose of an outline for people to remember what you said, to go away shaking their heads and saying "my what a sermon, what an outline, what a preacher"; or, is it simply for you to remember where you are in the sermon? Somehow I think it is and should be the latter. I go to conferences and conventions, and I hear more talk about how great the outline was than I do about the effectiveness of the message upon which the outline hung.

One of the more common mistakes in outlining is the overemphasis of alliteration. Everything doesn't have to rhyme. Everything doesn't have to have a sing-song way about it. Everything in the outline does not have to begin with the same letter. Sermons whose outline always begin with R or always begin with A frankly drive me crazy. I think we can be a bit fresher than that. That kind of preaching is not where it's at today. It is not what people listen to; not the medium through which they best receive truth. Don't overdo your outline. Remember this: You don't have to use alliteration in every outline. Every point doesn't have to begin with the same letter. In fact, if you do it only occasionally, it will be more effective when you do.

A further irritant in preaching is the overuse of the double outline. Rhyming outlines that sound like: "Consider the amazing claim of it, consider the agonizing concern of it, consider the awful crisis of it, consider the available compassion of it, and consider the awesome character of it." A-C, A-C, A-C, A-C. Sounds cute—but I promise you, to your hearers, that sing-song approach to outlining is more a negative than a plus. Beware of the overuse of alliteration, particularly the double alliteration and more.

2. Don't bring me up-to-date in your outline. Repetition can be good, but overusing repetition can be irritating. Many times, preachers will give their first point, then repeat it with their second point, then repeat the first two with the third point, and then repeat the first three with the fourth point. For example, "Consider the essential way of God's word." Preach a while and say, "Secondly, consider not only the essential way, but the eternal wonder of His Word," and then preach awhile. Then say, "Thirdly, consider not only the essential way and the eternal wonder, but the effective working of God's Word." Then preach awhile and say, "In conclusion, remember not only the essential way and the eternal wonder and the effective working, but the excellent wisdom of God's word." A bit nauseating? Enough said.

3. Get with it in your illustrations. Let's be specific. Number one, use plenty of illustrations. Two or three are not enough. Four to six or more would be better. Jesus was a master storyteller. He told about 35 stories which we call Parables. They were powerful idioms of truth. They more effectively conveyed, than anything He said, what Jesus was telling us. Next time you tell a story in a sermon, read your audience. Immediately—though some have been winding their watch, yawning or writing in their bulletin—every eye will be focused upon you and everyone will become dead still. Stories grab us, and we fail to be at our best if we do not follow the example of the Master in this way.

Further, use up-to-date stories. Many of you have an illustration library with nothing but old antique books of a hundred years or more. Don't tell me stories about Lord Fauntleroy, Victor of Aldersgate, or King What-his-name in the Battle of Someplace three hundred years ago. Read USA Today, everyday. Read World Magazine. Read your local newspaper. Listen to the evening news. Hear a major local news broadcast and national news broadcast once every day, five days a week. Tell a story three hundred years old, and some of your people will tune you out. But tell a story that everyone is familiar with, that everyone read in yesterday's newspaper that's all over TV, and use it to illustrate a Spiritual truth, and you will grab every listener by the heart.

Further, use good personal illustrations. Certainly confessional preaching is not everything, and all personal illustrations are not confessional. But when we do use a personal story that makes us look bad or foolish, or exposes our weaknesses, we immediately relate to people, who see a vulnerability, believability and integrity about us that makes us believable and relevant in our preaching. But remember this: ANY FAIRLY GOOD STORY THAT ACTUALLY HAPPENED TO YOU IS BETTER THAN A REALLY GREAT STORY THAT HAPPENED TO SOMEONE ELSE.

Also, consider expanding your sermon illustration source beyond books, papers, television, personal and real life, to other sources you may have not considered. Tony Evans is one of the most brilliant preachers in America. He preaches weekly on 600 radio stations on "The Urban Alternative" from Dallas, Texas. One of the many times he preached in our church at First Baptist Houston, we were talking about preaching, and he made a statement I have never forgotten. He said, "John, I believe that in the natural order of things, God has set an illustration for every Spiritual truth in the Word of God." "Illustrations," he continued, "don't have to be stories. They can be illustrations from natural order. How a star burns itself out, how an elevator must go up before coming down, etcetera." Jesus used these kind of illustrations as well as parables. Listen as He says, "Consider the lilies of the field, how they grow. They toil not, neither do they spin. Yet your Heavenly Father careth for them." When I read that, and thought about what Dr. Evans had said, I began to think. How do lilies grow? As I researched I learned that all plant life have three "tropisms." A tropism is a tendency toward; a tendency to seek. All plants have hydro-tropisms, the tendency to seek water. All plants have photo-tropisms, the tendency to seek light. They also have thermo-tropisms, the tendency to seek heat. Isn't that how we grow? By seeking the Light of the World, the warm heat of fellowship with Christ, and the water of the Word? Consider the lilies of the field. Get with it in your illustrations, and throw away some of those old, old illustration books.

4. Don't use so many notes. I want to wave the flag for the effectiveness of preaching without notes. When you use other people's material, and primarily only parrot the words of others, it is difficult to memorize. But when the material is yours, it has been birthed by the Holy Spirit in your heart, and you have written it yourself, the truth is, you probably already know it and don't realize it. The next time you finish a sermon you have written completely as your own, close your eyes and begin to preach it out loud. You will probably be surprised to find that you remembered 90% of it. If you will condense your sermon into a few key words—I usually have from 40 to 70—and memorize them, you will not only find it is much easier than you think, but that the effectiveness of your communication of the Gospel will be expedential.

There are three reasons why preaching without notes is of great value. First, the sense of authority and confidence that you have in your delivery is amazing. When you use notes, particularly a full set or manuscript, every time you have to look down, you acknowledge in your spirit and your delivery that you are the servant of those notes; you are chained to them; they are the master and you are the slave. When you have no notes, the material you have memorized in your heart is your slave; it is your servant and you are the master. Your sense of confidence and authority goes through the roof.

Also, when you preach without notes, your eye contact is 100%. Looking at the people—moving your eyes from person to person, reading the congregation and sensing what's going on—is an important tool in effective communication, particularly in preaching the Word of God. Eye contact is virtually lost when you use notes, particularly if you read a manuscript. It's easier than you think, and better than you can imagine.

Another great blessing I have found in preaching without notes is that often I struggle just for a second to think of something that I couldn't remember and the Holy Spirit brings something to my mind I hadn't planned to say. This often happens when I preach the same sermon in two services back to back. There was someone in the first service who didn't need something that I wasn't going to say, and God blocks it out. But He doesn't block it out in the second service. Or He may bring something to mind I hadn't planned to say for someone who needs it in the second service who was not in the first service. Preaching without notes allows the Holy Spirit of God to do that, and it makes you a far more effective communicator.

Try preaching without notes. Now, you don't have to do it all at once. Do a short sermon. Preach it in a Sunday school class, in a jail or at a small community gathering. Then work up and begin to eliminate a few more notes every time you preach. It is said that once every week at Metropolitan Tabernacle, Charles Haddon Spurgeon preached not only without notes, but spontaneously. Just before his message he would ask his music leader to give him a sermon idea, and he would preach totally extemporaneously. What a way to keep yourself sharp and your mind creative! Try it some time (when there are not too many people present).

5. Don't shout at me. For the last 50 years Americans have primarily received information from a 24 x 36 inch tube we call the television. That little screen is the means of communicating one-to-one that has impacted American thinking more than perhaps anything else. On the T.V. screen one person normally is talking to another. And notice that I said talking, not shouting.

For years, I really didn't know who I was as a preacher. If I heard Angel Martinez last, my delivery style was like Angel's. If it was Billy Graham or W. A. Criswell or Hyman Appleman or R.G. Lee, it was like them. Frankly, only about 15 years ago, I discovered the real me. I became conversational. And the effectiveness of my communication and response from my hearers was most encouraging.

Eight years before I retired, we began a contemporary service. I announced there would be skits, informal dress, guitars, contemporary music, etc. Our young people and young adults, single and married, were very excited. One day, a delegation of ten young adults came to see me. They said, "Brother John, we're really excited about the service, the music, the environment and everything. But we want to talk to you about your preaching." I said, "Lay it on me." They said, "First of all, we urge you to be a bit more conversational. Secondly, use more illustrations. Third, don't preach quite so long" (More about that in a minute). I took their advice. Immediately—immediately—I changed my style. Beginning the next Sunday, I used more stories, I preached shorter, and I was conversational. The attendance in that service increased weekly in an unbelievable way, as did the attendance in the older, traditional service. Trust me; this kind of preaching is where it's at today.

6. Don't preach so long. Through the years I have averaged 42 to 48 minutes in my sermons, including 12 to 18 minutes in the introduction. When I began preaching shorter, I began preaching better. Let's think again about television. This overwhelming influence in our society has dictated the 30-minute medium of communication. People are accustomed to listening and thinking in 30-minute segments. With commercials that's only about 25 minutes of content.

I made the decision to go from averaging 45 minutes to averaging 25 to 28 minutes and immediately became a better preacher.

Some years ago Doug Price, our T.V. and Media Director, began pleading with me to preach shorter so we could get the whole sermon on T.V. Our television program was always running off the air with the T.V. audience complaining that they missed the last part of my message. I tried, with some reluctance, but was rather unseccessful. One day he came to my office again and said, "Brother John, I want you to look at something." He showed me a 26-minute video of last Sunday morning's sermon. "How did you like it?" he said. "Pretty good, Doug," I responded, "better than I remembered." Then Doug told me something astounding. He said, "That was your 45-minute sermon. But I took out the repetition, the redundancy, the irrelevant, the unnecessary, and condensed it down to 26 minutes, and you didn't even realize it." I couldn't tell he had left out a thing. It was not only as good; it was better.

Shorter is better, and if you work harder, you can preach the same effective message and get better concentration from your people with a shorter delivery time. Preaching shorter is harder. You have to consolidate, eliminate and work; and say it sharper, better, more quickly and more effectively. To condense a sermon is much harder than to expand one. Filler is easy; quality and class are difficult. Someone said, "If you want me to preach an hour, I'm ready right now. If you want me preach 12 minutes it will take me a while to get ready."

7. Don't overlook the apologetic power of the Word of God. We know that the power is in God's Word. Billy Graham said, "If you have a lion, you don't need to defend him, just turn him loose and he'll defend himself." There's huge power in "Thus Saith the Lord" and simply quoting the Scripture. But if that's all we're supposed to do, why did God call us to be teachers? Certainly, a man who is explaining, doing exposition and apologetic of the Scripture he is teaching is going to be much more effective. Believe it or not, there are people in your congregation that don't believe a thing you say. And they are sitting there with their spiritual arms folded, saying, "Convince me."

As I listen to preaching today, and I listen to volumes of cassettes and CD sermons every month, I'm impressed with two things: the lack of the apologetic and the lack of application. Apologetics, of course, simply means to prove the logic of what you're saying. Argue your case; defend your position. Suppose I'm preaching, "Men are lost and going to Hell." I guarantee you, some people in my congregation are saying, "I simply don't believe that. A good God wouldn't send anybody to Hell." So I'm going to say, "Some of you are saying, 'I can't believe in the kind of God who would do something like that.' Let me ask you this, my friend, what would the kind of God you could believe in do with this kind of human stain?" Revelation 21:8, "But the fearful, and unbelieving, and the abominable, and murders, and whoremongers, and sorcerers, and idolaters, and all liars shall have their part in the lake which burns with fire and brimstone. This is the second death."

Let's look at a little simple home-spun apologetic. You're telling me that everyone goes to Heaven. All right, suppose one day we're walking down the streets of Heaven and hear some guns going off and the "boom-boom" of canons and bombs falling. I say "What's that?" They say, "Well, everybody goes to Heaven, so Khrushchev's up here, Castro's up here, Hussein's up here, Napoleon's up here, Hitler's up here; they're all up here because, you see, everybody goes to Heaven." A few days later, I'm walking down the streets of Heaven, and I hear a siren go off. I say, "What's that?" "Well, that's the eleven o'clock curfew. You have to run for your life; you have to get home and lock the doors." "Well, why is that? I thought this was Heaven." "Yes, you see, but everyone goes to Heaven, so the rapists are up here, the muggers are up here, the arsonists are up here, the murderers are up here, and it's not safe in Heaven." Now that bit of simple apologetic can go a long way to enforce the logic; hence the belief; by the hearer of the reality of Hell. Surely, we don't expect God to run the next world with less sense than we run this world. We separate good from evil down here. Those who make the grades advance, those who don't repeat the course. We do not put people with contagious diseases in the ward with the newborn babies. We separate those who break the law from those who keep the law. Surely we don't expect God to run the next world with less common sense than we have run this one.

Again, remember, there is great power in the Word of God. Simply quoting a verse of Scripture ignited by the Holy Spirit results in a powerful effect in the heart of the hearer. But when that Word is presented with some apologetics—some arguments, some logic, some defense—I promise you it is even more effective. Don't forget the importance of the apologetic.

8. Don't hide your application. I said the two missing ingredients in preaching today are the apologetic and the application. Once again, when you're stating Biblical truth, the Holy Spirit, without any help from you, is applying it to the life of the hearer. He is convicting them of its value and its truth. But as with the apologetic, when you apply it and reinforce what has been said in the Word, your preaching is even more effective. And sadly, I hear very little application in today's pulpit. Many sermons leave me with what I call "THE GRAND SO WHAT." A man gives me a lot of information, he gives me a lot of Scriptures, he explains what they mean, and then he says, "Let us pray." And I'm sitting there, screaming out in my heart, "THEREFORE WHAT? APPLY IT TO MY LIFE!" That is essential.

One of the best ways to do this is to consider Principal Preaching. Principal Preaching is not the ONLY way to preach, it is A way to preach. It is yet another weapon in your arsenal for proclaiming the Word of God. I don't preach every sermon the same way. I don't preach at a Southern Baptist Convention like I preach at a Sunday school class. I don't speak at a football stadium evangelistic crusade the way I preach at a funeral. But the application to your congregation in any setting is critical. Try sometime a new way of outlining in which you simply make the application, which is a LIFE-RELEVANT BIBLICAL PRINCIPLE, the outline. See my book, "Principle Preaching."

In Principle Preaching, you do not do any less exposition. We are to be Bible-expositors. The Word of God is God-breathed, infallible and inerrant. No Scripture is up for private interpretation. It doesn't mean what it means to me, it means what it means. But that is in its exposition.

In the application of the Scripture, there may be a thousand applications. Remember again, every Scripture has only one correct interpretation, but it may have a thousand applications. To explain what it means is wonderful; to also explain how what it means applies to my life is even better. Please hear me carefully when I say I am not talking about Neo-Orthodoxy. Neo-Orthodoxy denies what the Bible says. I am saying that we believe what the Bible says, but also we apply it by telling the people what it is saying. What it says is changeless; what it is saying as it applies to our life is essential to applying the Word of God to people's lives. Neo-Orthodoxy would say the story of the Red Sea is not true. The principle that God delivers His people faithfully is true. That's not what I'm saying. I do not espouse Neo-Orthodoxy; I totally reject it. The conservative expositor and applicator says the story of the Red Sea is true—it is a literal, geographical, historical fact—and does exposition about the history, the meaning, etc. But then he applies that to the life of the hearer and says God will part Red Seas in your life and miraculously provide for your needs.

In Principle Preaching, yet another weapon in your arsenal, you simply make the principles the outline. Surely, we are not preaching sermons with no application. In most sermons, there is application of the Scripture, but it is hidden; buried somewhere down in the exposition. In Principle Preaching the expository preaching is supreme. There is no more or less time, effort, or priority given to expository preaching—the exposition of the Scripture—in Principle Preaching than in non-Principle Preaching. All Principle Preaching does is to take great expository preaching, draw out the three or four life application principles and make them the three or four word outline. If you do that, I promise you, you will be better heard and better remembered. For what good is it if a man looks at himself in the mirror, sees he has need, and then walks away and does nothing? What good is it if we are hearers of the Word and not doers also? And the people need it explained to them such that what they do is relevant to what they have heard.

Let me give you just a brief example of what I mean by principle preaching, where you make the principle the outline. Listen again to Joshua 1:1-6:

*After the death of the Lord's servant Moses, the Lord
said to Moses' helper, Joshua the son of Nun, "My servant
Moses is dead. So you and all these people get up and cross
the Jordan River to the land I am giving to the people of
Israel. I have given you every place where the bottom of
your foot steps, as I promised Moses. Your land will be from
the desert and from Lebanon as far as the big Euphrates
River. It will be all the land of the Hittites to the Great Sea
on the west. No man will be able to stand against you all the
days of your life. I will be with you just as I have been with
Moses. I will be faithful to you and will not leave you alone.
Be strong and have strength of heart. For you will bring the
people in to take this land which I promised to their fathers
to give them.*

The average sermon outline for this passage by most preachers
would be:

   I. Consider the call of Joshua
  II. Consider the commission of Joshua
  III. Consider the conquest of Joshua
  IV. Consider the courage of Joshua
  V. Ho-hum.

Now, if you preach that same text with the same exposition,
but simply change the points to principles at the beginning of each
section of the sermon, listen to how it comes to life (remember
these are not points, but principles—remember the point is now the
principle):

    Principle I. Don't get stuck in life's hallways. Most
people spend their lives stuck in the hallways between two
great rooms in their life: where they failed yesterday and
what they're always going to do tomorrow and never get
around to. God came to Joshua in verse 2, and said, "Moses
my servant is dead, THEREFORE ARISE, and lead these
people forward." Moses the man is dead, stand up on your

feet and go forward. You've got to go on with your life. He didn't tell him to mourn 60 days, go into hibernation for two years or go see a counselor. He said let's get on with life; there's work to be done. In preaching like this, you help your people who are frozen in the past or fearful of the future have the courage to get up and get moving.

Principle II. God's already been where you're going. In verse 3 He says, "Every place that the sole of your foot shall tread upon that have I GIVEN TO YOU." Notice he didn't say "I WILL give it to you," He says, "I've ALREADY given you." It's already done; the victory is assured. God has already been where you're going. God's already in your tomorrow. Yours is not to fight the battle and win the victory. Yours is to appropriate the victory that's already been won by Christ.

Principle III. God has a wonderful blueprint for your life. In verse 4, He outlines in great detail the Promised Land. It is specific to the north, east, south and the west. So God has a great plan for you; trust Him. Get up and move forward, get in the future and trust His hand.

Principle IV: Yesterday's faithfulness ensures tomor-row's victory. Read again verses 5-6. "As I was with Moses, so I will be with you. I will never forsake you. So be strong and of good courage." The same God who was faithful to Abraham, Moses, Isaac and Jacob will be faithful to you. That's your guarantee. The apostle Paul writes, "These things that happened in the Old Testament happened as an example to us; as an encouragement to us."

This kind of sermon with this kind of outline will be remembered and applied to their lives by people far more than the same old ten-two-and-four—"Consider the Call of Joshua, the Commission of Joshua, the Conquest of Joshua and the Courage of Joshua."

Rick Warren suggests that in each sermon we should do four things. First, state the principle. Second, explain the principle. That's when you do 10 or 12 minutes of expository preaching on each point. Third, apply the principle. Fourth, illustrate the principle — tell the story.

So the exposition of the Scripture is still 95% of the sermon; nothing changes there. Expository preaching is still our priority. Principle preaching simply REARRANGES the expository sermon and rather than hiding the application, moves it to the front where it becomes the outline. Again, Pastor Warren says, "A man ought to be able to come to hear me preach, take notes on my outline, go home and put it on the refrigerator with a magnet and say 'Now I can do that when I get to work tomorrow morning.'" The inimitable Manual Scott, said, "Preaching ought to be talk that can walk." "The disciples were not learned men; they were tax collectors and fisherman and rebels and rejects. They simply heard Jesus preach and re-preached Him." He used to say, "They say drink Hill's Brothers coffee, it's re-heatable — well, the preaching of Jesus was re-heatable; it was re-preachable. They just heard what He said and understood it so clearly and simply, that they went out and re-preached it. And the Kingdom of God grew."

I cannot overstate what I've said. The message must never change. The Bible is God's perfect, inerrant Word. The only sermon we have is Jesus Christ crucified, risen and coming again. Expository preaching is the only kind of preaching for today and always. I'm simply appealing for a bit of adjustment in our delivery and in the arrangement of the application, which I have found will make you a hugely more effective preacher. And remember, you're not preaching at conventions, you're not preaching at pastor's conferences, you're not preaching to impress other preachers; you're preaching to men and women who live in the everyday world, who struggle with life, and who have given you 30 minutes to hear what you've got to say with the hope that something will change their life and make it better. Give them the truth, but sharpen up the way you deliver that truth from the mound and pray with all your heart. I believe your best days in preaching may well be before you.

Chapter 9

Pastoral Personal Purity

You know the statistics as well as I. The ministry has the highest fallout rate — the worst casualty rate — of any profession. Many of you have heard me tell the story of my father-in-law encouraging me when I became engaged to his daughter. Dr. Beck said, "John, I'll be praying for you. It's a long, long way to the end. It's been my observation that only one in ten men who enter the ministry at age 21 are still in it at age 65." I didn't believe it. I didn't tell Dr. Beck, but I wrote down in the back of my Bible the names of 25 of my contemporaries; friends who were preaching revivals and pastoring churches who were my age. Through the years, they fell; they quit. One-by-one, I checked them off. Today I'm 73 years old, and 20 of the 25 did not make it to the end. Only five did — Ron Dunn, Charlie Graves, Jerry Autrey, Hal Brooks and Freddie Gage. Only Freddie is alive today. The other four are in Heaven; the other 20, the Lord only knows where.

How sad the story. Surveys say that 1500 men quit the ministry in all denominations every month. And one-half say they would if they could simply move to another job. A recent statistic came across my desk. I have not had time to verify it. I pray it is not true. "Only 1 in 5 are still in ministry eight years after graduating from seminary." On a recent trip to preach at the First Baptist Church of Moore, Oklahoma, I was welcomed by the Associate Pastor who drove me the short distance from the airport to the hotel. As a long-time

Okalahoma Baptist, I began asking him about some of my friends. What about so-and-so? What about this pastor, and how's that one doing? The first four men I asked him about were acquaintances. Sadly, he told me, one after one, that three of them were divorced and no longer in the ministry. I quit asking about my friends.

Every day there is a new story. A prominent pastor in Colorado trapped in a homosexual relationship. The Jim Bakker and Jimmy Swaggart scandals were just the tip of the iceberg, and the end is not yet. I am not happy about this. I do not rejoice. I have no sense of judgment or hostility toward them, for we too are not without sin and dare not cast the first stone. I have a great desire in my heart to help restore the fallen brother. We had a retreat center for many years, where we brought pastors in trouble and provided counsel and comfort. The dear Assemblies of God people have a division in their denominational structure for pastoral reclamation. God bless them for that. And it hurts us all so when it happens.

In the '50s, the number one most respected man in the community was the pastor. Today he is number 11 or number 12. People used to go to church believing the pastor to be a man of God. It had to be proven to them that he was not. Today it's different. The average lost person goes to church believing the pastor is not a man of God, and he has to prove that he is. Have you noticed how many pastors now appear on T.V. with their wives? And how many billboards and newspaper ads contain pictures of husband and wife? We are desperately trying to repair the image that has befallen us, but we shall on these pages look at an ounce of prevention, which may well be worth much more than the proverbial pound of cure.

Why did 20 of 25 friends fall? I think three reasons—I'm sure there are many more. One is because of money. Many, underpaid in ministry, began making money on the side, began looking for deals and became more enamored with the dollar than with the Lord. Many men fell because they became liberal in their theology, preached a gospel with no power and had no results, and their churches subsequently got smaller and smaller. They were disillusioned. They never reached that ministerial pot of gold at the end of the rainbow. They never became well known. They never built large churches. They were never famous. To the contrary, they went the opposite direction, became frustrated, disillusioned, and quit. But by far the most common reason for ministerial fallout was sexual impurity. Some surveys say as many one-half of all pastors may watch pornography on the internet. And one must wonder; if almost weekly, or certainly at least monthly, we hear another new story or two about a fallen pastor, how many does each one represent of which we never hear?

It has certainly not been my intent in these pages to solve all our problems and offer solutions to everything, but rather to make some suggestions that may help in a spot or two. I hope each of you have found something to strengthen your ministry. But I can find no greater joy than in knowing that you have been helped personally in this area of your life. Whether you were ever known or are unknown. Whether you ever preached at a state convention, or had 50 in Sunday school or 5,000 in Sunday school, is not important. That you honor Christ, live a life of purity and integrity, and preach His Word with fidelity and are faithful to the end—THAT is everything.

And so I want to offer you some suggestions for strengthening your marriage and keeping your heart pure.

1. Keep your love affair with Jesus hot and passionate. With all my heart, I believe that falling into pornography is a symptom of losing our passion for our wife. And losing our passion for her is only a symptom of having lost our passion for Jesus Christ. I find that people who lose their love for Christ lose their passion for everything. They don't love their country, they don't love their job, they don't love their ministry and they certainly don't love their wife as once they did. Your relationship to Jesus is everything. Yes, you have eternal security. Yes, you are in constant relationship with Him. But what about the fellowship? Is it just okay, or is it scintillating, alive and exciting?

The man who has fallen out of love with his wife has first fallen out of love with Jesus. Our Lord gave us a beautiful prescription that indicates this when he told the church at Ephesus what to do to fall in love again. The problem in Revelation 2 is found in verse 4. He compliments the church but then addresses the problem head on. "Nevertheless, I have somewhat against you, because you have left your first love." Having stated the problem, Jesus then moves to the solution. It is a beautiful remedy; I have found it to work with everyone with whom I have every counseled and if you have lost your passion for your wife, you will find help here. Listen to verse 5. "Remember therefore, from whence thou art fallen, and repent. And do the first works, or else I will come unto thee quickly, and I will remove thy candlestick out of its place except thou repent."

There are three ingredients in falling in love again with your wife. The first is REPENT. Frankly, I was a bit surprised to find that as a part of the solution. But Jesus does not deal with falling out of love as an emotional problem or a marital problem, but a spiritual one. What kind of word is repent? Certainly it is not a medical term: Take two repents with a glass of water and call me in the morning. Nor is it an athletic term: First down and three repents to go. No, it is clearly a theological term. It means to be sorry and to stop doing it; to turn away; to quit. Clearly Jesus is calling falling out of love with your wife a sin, and He emphasizes the same thing at the end of the verse. Twice, in the beginning and at the end, He says, "repent". If you are out of love with your wife, you are out of love with Christ. That is a sin of which you must repent. You must get back in the Word, get on your knees, get your prayer life turned up real, real high and start witnessing to everybody you see. If you don't get excited about Jesus, you'll never get excited about your wife. And if that's the case, you will get excited about someone else or something else—and it may well be pornography.

The second ingredient in falling in love again is to REMEMBER. Use the soul; repent of your sin. Use the mind; remember how it used to be. Remember and play over again in your mind those great old days when you first met your wife; when you were passionate about her; when you loved her; when you first proposed. Remember your wedding night, remember the honeymoon. Remember how it used to be. Think on those things. The mind is a great help. People come to me sometimes and say, "I've been thinking of getting a divorce." I say to them, "Well, stop thinking about it. Start thinking about saving your marriage." As a man thinketh in his heart, so is he.

So the recipe is repent—use the soul; remember—use the mind; and DO AGAIN THE FIRST WORKS. To "do again" simply means to use your will. You start acting like you did when you *did* love her. You used to open the door, call her everyday, bring her roses, say sweet things, do the dishes and treat her like a queen. If you'll start doing that like you used to, repent of the fact that you quit doing it, remember how it used to be and play those beautiful tapes in your mind, you can and will fall in love again. If you don't fall in love again with Jesus, you won't fall in love with your wife. And if you don't fall in love with her, you're headed for trouble.

2. Give a new commitment to early-morning prayer. I have found that 30 minutes to an hour or more in the Word and on my knees in prayer is the key to everything. Sing to the Lord, sing in your heart, read His Word and talk to Him. Read it and then listen. Don't just make your requests known unto God. Listen in your heart as the Holy Spirit makes His requests to you. A ruined ministry is a terrible thing, and it can last 10 or 20, 30, 40, 50 years. You will live with it forever. Those 30 minutes to an hour every morning are not nearly as long, but 10 times more important. You say, "I don't have the time to pray and read the Word in the morning." Pastor friend, you don't have time *not* to. It is the key to everything.

3. I suggest you never be alone with a woman if humanly possible. Don't get in the car with her. Don't be in your office with her alone with the door shut. Don't say "just this one time" or go to lunch and say "well, it's not important, nothing will happen and nobody will worry," etc. Never—never—be alone with a woman. Counsel with the door open. Dictate with the door open. Meet with a lady with whom you counsel or with whom you serve in your office with your door open. AND, SPEND TWENTY DOLLARS AND HAVE A WINDOW CUT IN THE DOOR OF THE OFFICE WHERE EVERYONE CAN CLEARLY SEE WHAT'S GOING ON. That may be the best twenty or thirty dollars you will ever spend in all your life.

4. Be accountable. I am not internet savvy; I don't even know how to turn it on. My wife does it for me. But they tell me that it is almost dangerous to get on the internet. There are 260 million websites dedicated to pornography. What an astounding fact! It's virtually impossible, I'm sure, to turn on the internet, do some work and not come across a pornographic website. Many of them are traps. Something else allures you. And you will run across it, I'm sure. Once that picture is implanted in your mind, Satan has a stronghold from which you may never recover. And once that has happened, you may be drawn to it again and again.

Here's how to keep that from happening. They tell me there's a program called Covenant Eyes, where you can make a pact with a friend you respect to check your activity history on the internet. Well, spend the money, buy the program and do it today! Be accountable. Make a pact with someone—a pact that you cannot break and get around.

5. Learn to talk to your wife. We're the only creatures on earth with the gift of verbal intelligent communication. And we're the ones who use it the least and talk the least. That woman to whom you are married is a beautiful, wonderful person. Do your really know her? My wife and I began a habit many years ago of spending three or four nights a week sitting on the couch with a dim light, just talking. An hour, hour and a half, two hours—we have this corny little phrase with which we start off these kinds of conversations: "Tell me about your hopes and dreams and plans for the future." I find her to be a fascinating woman—intelligent, caring, deep—and the more I know her, the more I love her. You will never love your wife passionately until you know her, and you'll never know her until you talk to her. And remember, if you don't love her, you will love something else that may ruin your ministry.

6. Learn to turn your head. Between your heart and your eyes, there's something called the NECK. It can save your life. Job said, "I have made a covenant with mine eyes; that they should not look upon a maid." Good going, Job. There are looks, and then there are *looks*. You can't help the first look. There's nothing as attractive as a beautiful woman. But you can help the second look. There's an old country song about a man having an affair with another woman, and he's singing to her, "When we meet on the street, just walk on by—but wait on the corner." You have to learn to walk on by and NOT wait on the corner. You can't keep the birds from flying over your head, but you can certainly keep them from building nests in your hair. David fell into great tragedy, murder, loss and heartache because of adultery. He committed adultery because he didn't turn his head. Walking on the rooftop, he saw a beautiful woman bathing and stopped and looked. Give the devil a second, and he'll take a lifetime. Give him an inch and he'll take a mile. David should have turned his head, kept on walking and said, "Lord, cleanse me, cleanse my mind and forgive me of that thought." But he didn't, he stopped, he hesitated, he looked — and he was dead.

I think it is significant that the first Davidic psalm of which we have record, Psalm 1:1, begins with, "Blessed is the man who WALKS not in the counsel of the ungodly, nor STANDS in the way of sinners, nor SITS in the seat of the scornful." See the progression: walk, stand, sit. The connection between walking by and sitting, a picture of being engaged in the situation, is standing — this is the key. That's the middle link that got him from walking to sitting. We have to learn not to stand, not to hesitate; no, not for a second.

7. Prioritize family time. Have a date night with your wife every week. Go to your kids' ballgames. Don't miss a school play. Be a faithful at little league. Run errands together; go places together; hold her hand as you do. I pastored a large church with many ministries and over a hundred staff members. I can tell you there was a constant pressure to prioritize. But long ago, I told the church my priority would be my wife and children. I may not make every engagement and I may not attend every meeting, service or gathering, because I will give priority to my family." Did they holler, "Stone him!"? No, they stood and cheered. That's what the people want, and that's what we need.

8. Attend at least one marriage retreat a year with your wife. Get away. Be anonymous if you must. Go casual, go to the mountains, go to the beach, hear a good speaker, get with other couples, spend time with each other and refresh your marriage.

9. Keep a picture of you and your wife on your wedding day and a picture of your kids on your desk. Few things can help keep your heart and mind more in line and more loyal than something like this simple thing. And by the way, aren't those pictures great?

10. Go to bed at the same time. People with problems with addiction to internet pornography tell me that this is constantly the avenue through which pornography begins and is cultivated. Don't stay up late at night. Don't watch late night T.V. after she's in bed. Don't keep working when she's asleep. You've got plenty of time through the day to get your work done. When it's time to go to bed, go to bed—together.

Dear pastor, I pray for you with all of my heart. I have never felt contempt or retribution or harshness against a fellow pastor who falls. There's not a man among us who is not a heartbeat away from the same failure. My heart breaks. I love them; I pray for them. I do anything I can to help them. It is one of the calamities of our time, and it is one which He who was tempted in all points like as are we, fully understands and is able to succor those who rest on His gentle breast. Dear pastor, remember, GOD LOVES YOU, YOUR FAMILY BELIEVES IN YOU, YOUR CHURCH TRUSTS YOU AND SOUTHERN BAPTISTS NEED YOU.

Chapter 10

Tithing and the New Testament Believer

Nowhere does the man in the Southern Baptist pew not "get it right" than in the area of the Christian and his money. More specifically, "TITHING." Tragically, many, if not most, of our contemporary churches never mention money at all—certainly not tithing. It is not considered seeker-friendly.

A few years ago I went to be interim pastor for a year at a wonderful contemporary church with a Sunday attendance of nearly 3,000. The church was hundreds of thousands of dollars behind in its budget—and oh, by the way, they had never heard a sermon on giving from the pulpit. When I preached on tithing, numbers of people came by and said, "That's the first time I have ever heard anything like that."

Contemporary churches say preaching on tithing is not seeker-friendly. Traditional churches say it's not New Testament. The purpose of this chapter is to show that virtually nothing is MORE New Testament than tithing. For the Jew to give more under the law than the Christian under grace is a DISGRACE TO GRACE. Listen to Jeremiah 31:33, "But this shall be the covenant that I will make with the house of Israel. After those days, saith the Lord, I will put my law in their inward parts and write it in their hearts. And I will be their God, and they shall be my people." In a sentence, God's plan for the law is much more than the letter of the law. Remember those two words, MUCH MORE. In Matthew 5:17 Jesus said, "Think not that I have come to destroy the law or the prophets; I have not come to destroy but to fulfill." To fulfill: TO FILL UP FULLY that which was not full, not complete.

There are three kinds of law: the moral law, the civil law, and the ceremonial law. And none of them were complete. They were inadequate, incomplete, a portion, a percentage, partial and prophetical preview of the whole. Jesus was the main event. Jesus neither destroyed the law, came to negate it, or nullify it. He authenticated the law, He validated the law, He completed, consummated, filled up, made whole and full that which was lacking and incomplete. He went BEYOND, exceedingly above any and everything in the law. He was MORE THAN the law, greater than the law.

To the very end the disciples did not get it. Just before the ascension they said "Lord, will you at this time restore the Kingdom to Israel?" He taught them over and over again that Kingdom values are quite different than earthly ones. In fact, He said the Kingdom of God is not earthly at all; the Kingdom of God is within you. They looked for the Savior to come riding on a white horse, overthrow the Roman Empire and establish the physical, forceful monarchy of the Kingdom of Israel in their lifetime. When He went back to Heaven without doing so, they were still confused.

Just so today, many people are confused about the issue of the law. I want us to see that in each of the three kinds of law, the key phrase is MORE THAN. Jesus fulfilled them, went beyond, did MORE THAN, exceeded the law. IN EVERYTHING HE SAID, DID OR TAUGHT, JESUS EXCEEDED THE LAW. Remember those two words: MORE THAN.

Consider first the MORAL LAW—The Ten Commandments. The First Commandment says, "Thou shalt have no other God before Me." Jesus went beyond that and said, "I am God. I and the Father are one. They that have seen Me have seen the Father." It was a concept that had never been taught before.

The Second Commandment says, "Thou shalt not make unto Me any graven image. Nothing of wood or stone." But Jesus taught that loving family, land, possessions, friends or positions more than loving Him is worse than a graven image. It is idolatry of the very worst kind.

The Third Commandment says, "Thou shalt not take the name of the Lord thy God in vain." It was common among the Jews to make an oath in God's name. Jesus said, "Do not swear in the name of God; in fact, don't even swear by Heaven or by earth, for Heaven is God's throne and the earth is God's footstool; nor by Jerusalem for it is the city of the great King." He created them all. He exceeded the third commandment and simply said, "If you mean yes, say yes; if you mean no, say no. And swear by nothing at all."

The Fourth Commandment says, "Remember the Sabbath day, to keep it Holy." Jesus said He was Lord of the Sabbath. He did good on the Sabbath. He healed on the Sabbath. He took corn from the field and fed the hungry disciples on the Sabbath. He taught, "Man is not made for the Sabbath; he is not its servant. The Sabbath is made for man; it is *his* servant. And it is always right to do good on the Sabbath."

Jesus exceeded the law in the Fifth Commandment. "Honor thy mother and thy father." The Jews had a custom called "CORBAN." It was the practice of not giving money to needy parents by withholding the money in the name of God, saying it was CORBAN, special money dedicated to God. Jesus taught that to neglect one's parents in so doing is to dishonor God.

The Sixth Commandment says, "Thou shalt not kill." Jesus taught that a man could kill without committing the physical act. He said if you hate your brother, you have murdered him in your mind.

Everything He said was more than the law. He fulfilled the law. He went beyond the law and completed it.

The Seventh Commandment says, "Thou shalt not commit adultery." Jesus said, "He that looks upon a woman with lust in his heart, has committed adultery with her already in his heart." Jesus went beyond the law, it is always MORE THAN.

The Eighth Commandment says, "Thou shalt not steal." Jesus taught that stealing is more than taking a man's money. One can steal his reputation. One can destroy another's life by bearing false witness.

The Ninth Commandment speaks clearly to the issue of a false witness: "Thou shalt bear no false witness. Thou shalt not lie." Jesus went beyond simply talking about telling the truth; HE LIVED THE TRUTH. HE WAS THE TRUTH He completed the law. He said for all eternity, "I am the Way, the Truth, and the Life." He was ultimate truth. He did not just come as an example for telling the truth; he *was* the Truth.

The Tenth Commandment says, "Thou shalt not covet." The apostle Paul wrote that Jesus did not commit the ultimate act of covetousness in his own life. He did not count it something to be clung to or coveted to be equal with God. But Jesus laid aside His glory in Heaven, came to earth as a man in the form of sinful human nature, and died on the cross. He said to the Pharisees, "Which of you convict of me of sin?" His life was lived openly and within the scrutiny, gaze and judgment of all. These things were not done in a corner. No man ever convicted Jesus of sin. He lived His life yet without sin, that He might be the propitiation for our sin. In every case, not only did He keep the moral law, He exceeded it and went beyond it. Remember again those two words: MORE THAN.

The second kind of law is the CEREMONIAL LAW—how we relate to God. Again, in every point of the ceremonial law, Jesus went beyond. Within the ceremonial law were of course many ceremonies: feasts, ordinances, special days, sacrifices, festivals, celebrations, buildings and temples. But the elements of the cere-monial law were not an end in and in themselves. They pointed to Christ. They were previews of the coming attraction. Jesus said, "Search the Scriptures; they are they which testify of Me." The Old Testament contains Christ; the New Testament explains Christ. The Old Testament veils Christ; the New Testament unveils Christ. The Old Testament conceals Christ; the New Testament reveals Christ. The Old Testament promises Christ; the New Testament presents Christ. In the Old Testament, Jesus is the preview of coming attrac-tions. In the New Testament, He is the main event.

The Jews revered Solomon's temple. Jesus said, "Behold, a greater than Solomon is here." 70 years went into constructing the building. But He said, "I'm greater than that temple. Destroy the temple of My body, and in three days God will raise it up again."

But nothing more vividly shows the fulfillment and surpassing of the ceremonial law than the ceremony called the "Day of Atonement." On that day through the centuries, many lambs—millions, perhaps billions—were sacrificed for the sins of the world. They were male, young and spotless. When Jesus came, the male, young, spotless, perfect One, John the Baptist introduced His public ministry to the world in John 1:29 saying, "Behold THE Lamb of God which taketh away the sin of the world." The word THE is a definite article in the Greek. It denotes specificity and exclusivity. He is the specific One. He is the One and only specific Lamb of God to take away the sin of the world. He goes beyond all the millions. No more need for sacrificial blood on Jewish altars slain. The sacrifice is complete. Jesus paid it all. He is the one and only Lamb of the world. He is MORE THAN all the others combined and the consummate conclusion of all.

Jesus is greater than the altar. Hebrews tells us He sanctified the altar with His own blood. Jesus was the Lamb and the Altar. Jesus was our High Priest. Earthly men from the tribe of Levi for centuries paraded into the temple, behind the veil, to make atonement on the highest of Holy days for the sins of the people. But Jesus was forever our High Priest. He was after the order of Melchizedek. He was eternal, without beginning and without end of days.

Jesus is greater than the mercy seat. When the priest placed the blood on the mercy seat behind the veil in the temple, atonement was made for a whole year for the sins of the people. But this man Jesus, after He sacrificed His blood on the cross, ascended into the Holy of Holies not made with hands, placed His blood on the mercy seat and forever sat at the right hand of the Father. Once for all it was done. No annual repetition was necessary. It was completed. He exceeded both the blood and the mercy seat of the ceremonial sacrificial system.

The mercy seat was placed atop the Ark of the Covenant behind the veil of the temple. It was there that two golden angels faced each other, looking downward toward the golden bowl, the mercy seat, where the high priest placed the blood for the sins of the people. The mercy seat was attached to the top of the Ark of the Covenant. The Ark of the Covenant was a wooden box carried by the children of Israel in the wilderness by which the Lord guided them with His unerring hand through that long and perilous journey.

Inside the Ark of the Covenant were the Ten Commandments, God's LAW. Jesus fulfilled the law, and exceeded it, keeping every one and going beyond. Also, there was an opher, a small container of manna from the wilderness, indicating God's PROVISION. Jesus said, "I am the Bread of Life come down from Heaven." He taught us to pray, "Give us this day our daily bread." He is our Bread and our Provision. Also in the Ark was Aaron's rod, which bud, indicating God's POWER.

When Moses lifted his hands, the waters split. But Jesus surpassed the resurrection of the people of Israel to safe ground through the passage of the water. When He raised His hands on the cross, the waters of death split. He arose from the grave three days later and said, "I am the Resurrection and the Life. He that believeth in Me, though he were dead, yet shall he live." Jesus IS the Life. Jesus IS the Resurrection. He parted the waters of sin, death, Hell and the grave and rose from the dead that first Easter morning.

When Jesus died on the cross and said, "It is finished," the veil of the temple separating God and man split. There is now no separation from Jesus. WE have constant, perfect fellowship with Him. He IS the Altar, He IS the Priest, He IS the Sacrifice, He IS greater than the ceremonial law. He fulfilled the law; it is complete in Him. MORE THAN, MORE THAN, MORE THAN!

As the ceremonial law demonstrates how we relate to God, the CIVIL teaches how, rightly related to God, we now relate to each other. Listen to the revolutionary teaching of Jesus in Matthew 5:21-47:

> *Ye have heard that it was said of them of old time, Thou shalt not kill; and whosoever shall kill shall be in danger of the judgment: But I say unto you, That whosoever is angry with his brother without a cause shall be in danger of the judgment: and whosoever shall say to his brother, Raca, shall be in danger of the council: but whosoever shall say, Thou fool, shall be in danger of hell fire. Therefore if thou*

bring thy gift to the altar, and there rememberest that thy brother hath ought against thee;

Leave there thy gift before the altar, and go thy way; first be reconciled to thy brother, and then come and offer thy gift.

Agree with thine adversary quickly, whiles thou art in the way with him; lest at any time the adversary deliver thee to the judge, and the judge deliver thee to the officer, and thou be cast into prison. Verily I say unto thee, Thou shalt by no means come out thence, till thou hast paid the uttermost farthing.

Ye have heard that it was said by them of old time, Thou shalt not commit adultery: But I say unto you, That whosoever looketh on a woman to lust after her hath committed adultery with her already in his heart.

And if thy right eye offend thee, pluck it out, and cast it from thee: for it is profitable for thee that one of thy members should perish, and not that thy whole body should be cast into hell. And if thy right hand offend thee, cut it off, and cast it from thee: for it is profitable for thee that one of thy members should perish, and not that thy whole body should be cast into hell.

It hath been said, whosoever shall put away his wife, let him give her a writing of divorcement: But I say unto you, That whosoever shall put away his wife, saving for the cause of fornication, causeth her to commit adultery: and whosoever shall marry her that is divorced committeth adultery.

Again, ye have heard that it hath been said by them of old time, Thou shalt not forswear thyself, but shalt perform unto the Lord thine oaths: But I say unto you, Swear not at all; neither by heaven; for it is God's throne: Nor by the earth; for it is his footstool: neither by Jerusalem; for it is the city of the great King. Neither shalt thou swear by thy head, because thou canst not make one hair white or black. But let your communication be, Yea, yea; Nay, nay: for whatsoever is more than these cometh of evil.

Ye have heard that it hath been said, An eye for an eye, and a tooth for a tooth: But I say unto you, That ye resist not evil: but whosoever shall smite thee on thy right cheek, turn to him the other also. And if any man will sue thee at the law, and take away thy coat, let him have thy cloak also. And whosoever shall compel thee to go a mile, go with him twain.

Give to him that asketh thee, and from him that would borrow of thee turn not thou away.

Ye have heard that it hath been said, Thou shalt love thy neighbour, and hate thine enemy. But I say unto you, Love your enemies, bless them that curse you, do good to them that hate you, and pray for them which despitefully use you, and persecute you; That ye may be the children of your Father which is in heaven: for he maketh his sun to rise on the evil and on the good, and sendeth rain on the just and on the unjust.

For if ye love them which love you, what reward have ye? Do not even the publicans the same? And if ye salute your brethren only, what do ye more than others? Do not even the publicans so?

In Jesus' day, the Roman Empire required a citizen in an occupied country to carry the pack for any Roman soldier walking by for one mile. Jesus said if any man requires you to go one mile, go with him two miles. If a man requires your coat, give him your cloak. If he smites you on one cheek, turn the other cheek. Bless them that curse you. Pray for them that hate you and spitefully use you. If your brother has something against you, reconcile to him, and don't just wait for him to reconcile to you. You actually go beyond the need to forgive when he asks you to forgive. YOU INITIATE the reconciliation and forgiveness on both parties whether or not you are guilty. This was far, far beyond anything the law had ever said or they had ever imagined.

The law said you are to forgive a man three times. Peter, wanting to impress the Lord, doubled it, and threw in one for good measure. "Lord, how many times shall I forgive my brother? Seven times?" he asked. Jesus answered, "No, seventy times seven." Did Jesus mean forgive 490 times, and then on the 491st time you do not forgive?

No. It was simply a metaphor in which He was saying you never stop forgiving. He went beyond the law. Forgiveness is much more, far MORE THAN anything they had ever seen or heard.

The Roman law said to pay your taxes. The Jews refused and said, "We honor no one but God, and give only money to the temple." Jesus said no, it's MORE THAN that: "Render unto Caesar the things that are Caesar's and unto God the things that are God's."

The law said you could put away your wife with a writ of divorcement for any cause. Jesus said "No, it's more than that." The only cause for divorce is adultery. He who marries her that is divorced for any other reason commits adultery.

The Old Testament sums it all up. "Thou shalt love the Lord thy God with all mind and thy heart and thy soul." Jesus said this was the greatest commandment, and added the golden rule "Do unto others as you would have them do unto you." Again, the teaching is clear. MORE THAN, MORE THAN, MORE THAN. He came to fulfill the law; he went beyond the law and made it complete. It was not complete, it was not fulfilled; it was only partial and incomplete.

I have an important question for you. If Jesus exceeded the law in everything he said, taught or did; if the heart of His entire life and ministry was more than, more than; how can you believe this includes everything BUT that which may well be the most important thing in the Christian life—OUR STEWARDSHIP, OUR GIVING? Remember for a Jew to give more under the law in a simple tithe than the Christian under grace is a DISGRACE TO GRACE.

On what basis do I say that our relationship to money may well be the most important thing in the Christian life? For starters, Jesus said, "Where your treasure is, there will your heart be also." That verse is often misquoted. Many people say, "Where your heart is, there your treasure be." But the truth of the matter is, they're both in the same place. You cannot love God with all your heart and not love Him with all your treasure.

Two entire books of the New Testament, 1 John and James, were written to say our life, our actions and our works validate the reality of our profession of faith. We can talk a good game, but unless we DO there is no salvation. Our good works do not contribute to our salvation, but they ARE the major reality which validates its authenticity. Far short of contributing to one's salvation, Jesus paid it all and by grace we are saved through faith—*not* by our works. But where there are no works, faith without works is dead. Faith that produces no works is empty faith. Faith that produces good works demonstrates it is real faith.

And what is the most difficult of all human works for most believers? Is it not the giving of our money? Is it not the most significant indicator of our relationship to Christ? Is it not that which means the most to us? We work hard for it—for our retirement, for our savings, for our family, our food, our clothing, our shelter, our home, our children's education, our car, our vacations, our fun and our holidays. Of course, it is central to our lives. Jesus reversed all that and said "Look," in Matthew 6:33, "if you will simply put me first, I will give you all those things. Seek all of these things and you will lose your soul." But seek the Lord Jesus Christ and His Kingdom first, with all your heart and soul, and everything, all these things will be added unto you.

How important is our money? It is probably the ultimate measurable indicator of our spirituality.

- There are 2250 verses in the Bible about money.
- More is said in the New Testament about our relationship to our possessions than is said about prayer, Hell and faith combined.
- The number one theme of the parables is our relationship to our money.
- STEWARDSHIP IS THE NUMBER TWO THEME OF THE NEW TESTAMENT, SECOND ONLY TO SALVATION.

It is clearly the consummate validator of our profession and measurement of the authenticity of faith. Jesus told the rich young ruler that he must leave everything to be His disciple. I am Jesus' disciple, but I did not leave everything, because my possessions were not more important to me than God. But Jesus read the heart of the rich young ruler and knew that to him his possessions were everything. And he went away sadly, refusing to follow Christ because they were more important than Him. In all of life, if anything is more important to you than Christ, you cannot be His disciple. And in all of our lives, the single most important thing to the unspiritual person is his physical possessions and well-being.

Let me finish with a question, the answer of which is self-obvious. If Jesus exceeded the law, went beyond the law, fulfilled the law; if the essence of His life was MORE THAN, MORE THAN, MORE THAN; and everything He ever said, taught or did, of which we have a record, exceded the law—the moral law, the ceremonial law and civil law—do you believe He did not intend for us to do the same in the most important thing: giving? 10%—that's just for starters. That's for the beginner; that's Old Testament. But He exceeds the Old Testament, He fulfills the law, and that not only includes but also prioritizes the number two theme of the New Testament next to salvation; our relationship to our money. Remember again, for the Jew to give more under the law than the Christian gives under grace is a DISGRACE TO GRACE.

Chapter 11

The Private Prayer Language – Part 1

God promises no physical evidence of the "filling of the Spirit" except power to be His witnesses. God fills in response to faith as repentance and surrender make possible the overflow of the Holy Spirit that dwells within. At the heart of Charismatic theology, however, is the erroneous teaching that the exclusive way by which one knows that he is "filled with the Spirit" is that he speaks in a kind of garbled utterance referred to as "speaking in tongues," an experience over which the "tongue speaker" virtually has no control. To correct this error, the question must be addressed, "Precisely what is the meaning and the purpose of the spiritual gifts?"

Spiritual gifts are a Holy Spirit-given, Holy Spirit-bestowed propensity toward the accomplishment of the work of God on earth, and each is not necessarily for everyone. All gifts are not given to all men. The Holy Spirit gives to each of us individual gifts, severally, as He will. The various GIFTS of the Spirit are intended to create the **ministry** of Jesus — what He did — just as the FRUIT of the Spirit is to create His **character** — what He was like.

To understand Spiritual gifts it is essential to understand that there are three categories of gifts:

I. The Gift Of The Gifted Person — According to Ephesians 4, when Jesus ascended into Heaven, He gave the church, His body, certain gifts to bring His people to the unity of the faith and the full measure of the stature of Christ.

*Wherefore he saith, When he ascended up on high, he
led captivity captive, and gave gifts unto men: (Now that he
ascended, what is it but that he also descended first into the
lower parts of the earth? He that descended is the same also
that ascended up far above all heavens, that he might fill all
things.) And he gave some, apostles; and some, prophets;
and some, evangelists; and some, pastors and teachers; For
the perfecting of the saints, for the work of the ministry, for
the edifying of the body of Christ: Till we all come in the
unity of the faith, and of the knowledge of the Son of God,
unto a perfect man, unto the measure of the stature of the
fullness of Christ: From whom the whole body fitly joined
together and compacted by that which every joint supplieth,
according to the effectual working in the measure of every
part, maketh increase of the body unto the edifying of itself
in love.*

Ephesians 4:8-13, 16

Among those gifts, He gave some apostles—the foundational
ministry of the church, prophets (or proclaiming preachers), evangelists and teaching pastors. The expression in Ephesians 4:11,
"Pastors and teachers" simply means "pastor-teachers" or "pastors
who teach." The first category of spiritual gifts is THE GIFT OF
THE GIFTED MAN OR WOMAN THEMSELVES, the sense in
which the individual themselves, while they will possess the gift,
ARE the gift. Billy Graham, for example, is a gift of God to the
church to help us do the works of evangelism.

II. The Sign Gift to The Unbeliever—Before New Testament
canon was completed, it was God's way to validate the authenticity
of the Gospel message by the working of signs. If two people come
to town today and preach two different messages, I may simply open
the pages of the New Testament and determine which one is telling
the truth by the New Testament. During the Apostolic Era, however,
before the New Testament was completed, there was no such vali-
dating authority. During this particular time in history, God used
signs and miracles to authenticate the apostolic ministry and message
of the crucified carpenter of Nazareth. But if our two preachers with

two opposing messages have no accompanying written authority, I am likely to believe the one who can raise the dead and make blinded eyes see. This principle is as old as time itself. God gave Pharaoh miracle after miracle to validate His Word and authenticate the fact that it was He who was behind the command, "Let my people go."

In the New Testament the practice continued. Jesus bemoaned the faithlessness of Israel and said, "Except ye see signs and wonders, ye will not believe." Paul added, quoting the prophet Hosea, that even though God works miracles in the face of Israel, "YET THEY WILL NOT BELIEVE." Paul validates his own ministry by reminding them that the "signs of an apostle" were done among them (II Corinthians 12:12).

The Jews regularly demanded of Jesus proof of His authenticity. Hear them as they asked, "What sign showest thou unto us?" (John 2:18) Paul adds in I Corinthians 1:22, "The Jews REQUIRE a sign," and adds in I Corinthians 14:22, "Wherefore tongues are for a sign, NOT TO THEM THAT BELIEVE, but to them that believe not."

One of the verses Charismatics most like to use to support their position is, in fact, a support of the truth we are sharing in this chapter. In the closing verses of Mark 16, Jesus said,

> *And These signs shall follow them that believe; In My name shall they cast out devils; they shall speak with new tongues: They shall take up serpents; and if they drink any deadly thing, it shall not hurt them; they shall lay hands on the sick, and they shall recover.*
> Mark 16:17-18

Mark's closing comment is:

> *So then after the Lord had spoken unto them, he was received up into Heaven, and sat on the right hand of God: And they went forth, and preached everywhere, the Lord working with them, and CONFIRMING the word with signs following. Amen.*
> Mark 16:19-20

This controversial passage does not support Charismatic theology as Charismatics suppose. Precisely the opposite is true. The expression, "follow them that believe" literally means "breathing in an atmosphere." In other words Jesus is saying, "Those who believe will be believing in an atmosphere of the miraculous." As we have said, the passage closes with the precise purpose of the signs that were the atmosphere in which converts believed—SIGNS CONFIRMING THE WORD. The Apostolic Era, approximately 33 A.D. to 90 A.D., was characterized by miraculous signs confirming the Word. As the Apostolic Era wound down and New Testament canon came into existence, the written Word was available to authenticate the ministry and the message of the Apostles. Subsequently, history verifies a tremendous slowing, if not complete cessation, of this dynamic method of confirming the Word by the use of "sign gifts" to the unbelievers with the ability to perform miracles, cast out demons, speak in languages not learned and cure disease virtually at will. To this day, in many pagan countries where there is no faith in the message of the New Testament, it is not uncommon for missionaries to report that God still uses the method of miraculous signs to confirm the Word. But history reveals the more exposure people have to the Word, the less the need to validate its truth with miraculous signs. The Holy Spirit performs His own validation to the heart of the man who hears the Word.

III. Edifying Gifts For The Sake Of The Body—The second category of sign gifts to unbelievers, namely miracles, exorcism, languages, and healing was intended for the UNBELIEVER. The third category of gifts, like the first, is intended for the BELIEVER. In the fourteenth chapter of John, Jesus taught that the world would not believe the Gospel because they would see Him no more (John 14:17), for the world doesn't buy what it cannot see. Man with his humanistic approach to life will naturally attempt to explain the divine in terms of the human. Therefore, Jesus prayed in the garden that His followers would be one, in order that the world might believe Jesus came from God. What is Jesus saying? Simply this! The New Testament church, functioning in harmony with itself, joined fitly by the Spirit to the Head in Heaven, becomes His body on earth. Once He incarnated Himself for 33 years in a human body. NOW HE

PERPETUALLY INCARNATES HIMSELF IN HIS NEW BODY, THE CHURCH.

There are many analogies used by the Lord to picture the relationships between Christ and His own. He is the Shepherd, we are the sheep; He is the Foundation, we, the building; He is the Vine, we, the branches; He is the Groom, and we, the bride. None is more expressive, however, than the picture of Christ as the Head with all believers comprising His body on earth. The world does not see Christ, but it *may* and *must* see Him in us. A New Testament church acting in harmony with itself and with the corporate body of Christ on earth is His CONTINUING INCARNATION. Since the world is to see Christ in us, the Holy Spirit at conversion gives each Christian a spiritual body-edifying gift or two or more. These gifts are characteristics of Christ. They are gifts of mercy, exhortation (encouragement), helping, leading (administration), faith, giving—to name a few. No gift is greater than any other gift, and if one gift IS greater than another, it is the least attractive gifts that are the most important. Kidneys and livers are not as publicly attractive as beautiful hair and flashing eyes, but you can live without your eyes and hair more easily than you can live without your liver and kidneys. We are not to work for a gift, boast in a gift, make central a gift, or press the importance of one gift above another. We are to be thankful for whatever body-edifying gifts the Spirit has given us and use them.

In Chapter 14 of I Corinthians, Paul says that in spite of the sign of tongues the majority of Israel will not be saved. I Corinthians 14:21-22 states, "In the law it is written, with men of other tongues and other lips will I speak unto this people; and yet for all that will they not hear me, saith the Lord." *"Wherefore, tongues are for a sign, not to them that believe, but to them that believe not; but prophesying serveth not for them that believe not, but for them who believe."* This simple and most authoritarian and concise doctrinal statement on this contemporary and difficult issue came from no less an authority than the inspired pen of the sainted apostle himself. It is a wonder to me that there could be any continuing confusion over the purpose and meaning of tongues. They were never intended to be the spiritual play-toy for believers they have become. As Christians, our relationship is centered not in emotion, not in experience but in faith—and a faith centered in the integrity of His Word. God is to be believed; God is to be taken at His Word. We have no need as Christians for signs to be an evidence of anything. That a large segment of the Christian body demands speaking in tongues as a sign that God has filled the believer with His Spirit is an expression of the immaturity of that portion of the church. Tongues are for a sign, NOT to them that BELIEVE, but to them that believe NOT!! It should be ludicrous to have to pursue the point further. The purpose of tongues is to be a sign to the unbeliever. And yet the doctrinal error that abounds in the land goes to a large degree unchecked in spite of the clear teaching of Scripture.

Chapter 12

The Private Prayer Language – Part 2

In this chapter, we shall attempt to answer a few simple questions as objectively as possible, relating to the issue of speaking in tongues. As we do so, let us remember our basic hermeneutical principles: language, grammatical, contextual, historical, literal, spiritual and synthesis.

   1. What Are Tongues? The word "tongues" is a Greek word "glossa" and is the normal Greek word commonly used for human language: languages such as French, German, or Russian. On the Day of Pentecost, devout men out of every nation under Heaven gathered in Jerusalem. The purpose of the gift was at once practical and obvious. They could not understand the Hebrew and/or Aramaic being spoken by the disciples and so we have believers testifying with words of other languages coming from their mouths. Each person heard in his own language the wonderful works of God. After Pentecost, the world travelers returned to their home countries and the process of world evangelism was begun. In our King James Version of the Bible you can find the word "unknown" before "tongues" italicized indicating that the word does not appear in the Greek and indeed, it does not. The New Testament never speaks of unknown languages. "Glossa," or "tongues," was always known languages. Linguists for decades have referred to languages as language families or kinds of language. There is no such thing as kinds of gibberish. It must always be referred to in the singular. New

Testament tongues were and are intended to be known languages used to speak the Gospel to an unbeliever in his own language.

In Acts 2:8 a different Greek word—"dialektos" is interpreted "language." This is the word from which we get "dialect." At Pentecost, people were in attendance from all over the world. Appropriately, the Holy Spirit gave them the message not only in the language of their country but also in their clearly identifiable dialect as well. How gracious of our Lord and how thorough!

Another word used in connection with languages or tongues is the Greek word "genos" meaning "kind." Paul uses it in I Corinthians 12:10 to refer to different kinds of tongues. The word refers to various families of languages, not gifts. Paul refers to the kind of gifts the pagans used in I Corinthians 14:10-11 as a warning that this unknown gibberish practiced in the church will be a testimony *against* the church rather than *to* the world, for they will surely think you are insane (verse 23). Let it be clearly understood that from Acts 2 forward, tongues were known languages, the practice of which was intended to confirm the authority of the Gospel to unbelievers.

2. Why Was the Gift of Languages Given? Paul's incessant answer is "tongues are for a sign." At Paul's own infilling, there were not tongues. He did not need the sign, for he already believed. Neither did Annanias who ministered to him. Annanias believed. Paul believed. They both believed. So at his filling of the Spirit, no sign was given, for no sign was needed (Acts 9:17-18).

3. What Is the New Testament Pattern for the Proper Use of the Gift of Languages? Certainly not I Corinthians! I Corinthians is the worst hodgepodge of immorality, doctrinal error, moral confusion, theological heresy, and social practice in the New Testament. The Corinthians had just come out of paganism, but not very far. They were saturated in it and influenced by it on every hand. Throughout this letter Paul makes a superhuman effort to attempt to straighten out the abuse of a beautiful gift. To attempt to build a theology on tongues from the book of I Corinthians is like learning to build a ship by looking at the twisted wreckage of an explosion. The Corinthian church was a wreck. There were divisions, cults, cliques, devious personalities and heresy in every quarter. It had sexual perversion, adultery, fornication, unbridled incest, worldliness and materialism.

Church members were taking each other to court. Apostolic authority was under siege. Failure to discern abounded. Confusion and misunderstanding were everywhere. There were abuses of theology, idolatry, self-love, pride, scandal and even demon worship. There were abuses of the intended roles of men and women in the church. There was doctrinal error in everything from the virgin birth to the resurrection. There were abuses at the Lord's Supper table with drunkenness, gluttony and the resultant judgment of the sin unto death.

Most graphically, there were abuses and perversions of the spiritual gifts—PARTICULARLY the gift of language. We would expect that the people who brought us "pride in open incest" in I Corinthians 5 might now bring us the jumbled mess in the rampant abuse of languages found in Chapters 12 and 14.

I Corinthians was a massive attempt to deal with the tragedy of the perversion of everything. It is of interest to note that the great 13th chapter on love is inserted between two strong teachings in Chapters 12 and 14. The Corinthians had managed to drag every aspect of their former pagan lives into the church, of which the abuse of the common gibberish spoken in pagan temples was the most obvious example.

The problem was not a lack of spiritual gifts. In chapter 1, verse 7, he says, "You are not lacking in any spiritual gift." The question was not the POSSESSION of the gift. It was the ABUSE of the gift. The issue was the *misuse* of the gift of language. Josephus reminds us that the "more wild and agitated they became, the more spiritual they believed themselves to appear to be." The desire to look spiritual was the reason the gift of language was so grossly perverted and exploited in Corinth. The simple, subtle temptation to instant spirituality may well be behind the parallel abuse of the gift today. A core of mature believers abode at Corinth, but the majority of the church saved out of paganism in this highly gentile city was at once immoral and downright heathen. In Corinth, paganism was spelled with a capital "P." So identifiable was she with sexual perversion and immorality that her name actually became a verb. "To Corinthianize" literally meant "to go to bed with a prostitute." Corinth was well known for her sin!

At every turn the background of the Corinthian believers worked against them. It was like trying to save a drowning man from a cesspool by throwing him a fragile, rubber raft filled with holes. We are not surprised that the great New Testament abuse of these sign gifts, couched against a background of ecstatic speech in pagan temple, abounded in the Corinthian church. In his attempt to straighten out the problem, Paul is not minimizing the gifts, nor am I. *He is attempting to correct the wrongful use of the gifts.* In his correction of them, he uses satire and ridicule along with logic and persuasion. He is dealing with them as babes, for babes they were.

The I Corinthians letter must *not* be used as a textbook on the proper use of the gift of languages. It is an analysis of a shipwreck whose value may best be understood in terms of "what not to do." The normal use of tongues may be clearly seen as a sign to unbelievers in the book of Acts. In Chapter 2 it is used to confirm the Gospel to the Jews on the Day of Pentecost. In Chapter 10 it is used to confirm the Gospel to the Gentiles. Cornelius, the captain of the Roman band, was a Gentile world traveler. The Jews at Pentecost spread over the world declaring the new message of the Gospel which had been confirmed by the gift of language. In Acts 10, Gentile Cornelius would travel the world as a Roman captain covering the world with the new message of the Gospel that had likewise been confirmed to him by the gift of languages (Acts 10:44-48). In Acts 8 we have a kind of Samaritan Pentecost when again the Gospel is preached and confirmed by the miraculous to yet another section of society, the half-Jew and half-Gentile. While this chapter does not specifically say that the event at Samaria was accompanied by the confirming gift of language, it does say it was confirmed by miracles and signs (Acts 8:13). We may assume that in keeping with the pattern of Acts, a part of those signs was the gift of language. The fourth and only other incident of the gift of languages in the pattern of Acts is in Acts 19. We have stated before that when the half message of Apollos was completed by the whole message of Paul to the Jews in Ephesus, the sign was again displayed. EVERY SEGMENT OF SOCIETY WAS INTRODUCED TO THE GOSPEL BY THE USE OF THE GIFT OF LANGUAGES AS A SIGN TO CONFIRM THE WORD. In Acts 2 it was to the Jews. In Acts 8 it is to the half-Jew. In Acts

10 it is to the Gentile. In Acts 19 it is to the full Jew who only had half a message. WITH THAT, THE ACCOUNT OF LANGUAGES IS CLOSED. THE NECESSITY IS OVER. THE DOOR OF THE GOSPEL HAS OPENED TO THE ENTIRE WORLD. Corinth is a picture of the mess that occurs when the gift is abused. Don't use the Corinthian church as a standard for the proper use of the gift of languages. That pattern is found in Acts and Acts alone.

4. When Will Tongues Cease? It is strange indeed to see that the practice of the gift of languages is on the increase as we near the end of the time when in fact the Scriptures said it would decrease and even stop. One must question why modern Charismatics are not in harmony with Biblical prophecy! Why do they perpetuate the abuses found in the church at Corinth? Does it surprise you that I raise the question, "When will it stop—when will tongues cease?" It shouldn't. Paul makes it clear that this gift will not go on forever. He has repeatedly asserted that it is one of the least of the gifts, with prophecy (preaching) being the most important. We shall see that he says tongues will stop before Christ's coming. How may Charismatics justify its increased use towards the end of time? We should not be surprised that the gift of language is not an eternal one. It will not operate until the end of time and will die out. If the gift of language is to die out before the coming of Christ, WHAT ARE MODERN CHARISMATICS PRACTICING TODAY?

Listen to Paul's incisive prophecy in I Corinthians 13:8-13: "Love never faileth; but whether there be prophecies, they shall be done away; whether there be tongues, they shall cease; whether there be knowledge, it shall vanish away. For we know in part, and we prophesy in part. But when that which is perfect is come, then that which is in part shall be done away. When I was a child, I spoke as a child, I understood as a child; but when I became a man, I put away childish things. For now we see in a mirror, darkly; but then, face to face; now I know in part, but then shall I know even as also I am known. And now abideth faith, hope, love, these three; but the greatest of these is love."

The verb "shall fail" used in connection with the failure of knowledge and the vanishing of prophecy or preaching are the same two verbs of the same Greek word "Katargeo"—"making or made to stop." It means that preaching and knowledge will stop because something will happen, forcing them to cease. The verb used in connection with tongues—tongues shall cease—is the Greek word "pauo", meaning "cease of themselves." This verb form means there is not an external action involved in their dying out, but that they die out from within. Something INTERNAL causes tongues to die out of themselves and end while something EXTERNAL is forced upon knowledge and preaching making them die out. Preaching and knowledge are made to stop. Tongues stop of themselves.

5. When Will All of This Occur? In context we see at the beginning of verse 9 the copulative "For" continuing and explaining the previous thought. The reason for the difference in the tongues fizzling out while preaching and knowledge are stamped out is that "that which is perfect (or complete) is come." Preaching and knowledge continue until the end of time and are forced to stop by the coming of Christ. In Heaven there is no more need to preach, for we are all saved and no more need the gift of knowledge, for "we shall know as we are known" (verse 12). But before the coming of Christ will make knowledge and preaching cease, Paul says tongues *will have died out by themselves.* Then what the Charismatics are practicing today is highly suspect at best. You may be assured that the coming of Christ with its subsequent glorious rapture of the believer to Heaven is that to which he refers. For when this happens, we shall see "him face to face" (verse 12). Just after the resurrection, at the rapture, we shall have complete knowledge, and will know as we are known. Let there be no question that Paul's statement, "When that which is perfect is come, then that which is in part shall be done away" does not refer to the completion of the New Testament canon. We have had the New Testament for 2,000 years and yet we have preaching and the need to learn and disseminate knowledge. NO! It is a clear-cut reference to the coming of Christ and the end of the world. By then, the great authority on the subject says tongues will have ceased.

There is no more beautiful gift when used as intended than the gift of speaking in languages not learned. In July 1971, we took 400 teenagers to the hills of West Texas for our first annual youth camp at First Baptist Church, Houston. One evening a lovely young lady named Sarah Morrow, a mature, Spirit-filled Christian, was standing under a tree witnessing to an Indian boy who was a devil worshiper. Suddenly words poured from her mouth she did not understand. When she finished, the Indian boy stepped back in surprise and said, "You just spoke to me in the Cherokee language." Sarah was surprised, but soon we rejoiced at the immediate conversion of the young man. This beautiful gift is still operating in the world, though it is dying out as the Scripture prophesied. It is a pity that the *abuse* of the gift is on the increase. Let there be a clarion call through the body of Christ to return to the proper use of this beautiful sign gift to an unbelieving world. Remember the gift may be counterfeited, so you must test it to see if it is real.

If you think you have it, walk along a seaport and witness to sailors coming off ships from all over the world. If you speak and Russians and Finns and Germans and Ethiopians hear in their language—you've got it! So use it like it is supposed to be used. DON'T SIT IN YOUR CLOSET AND ENTERTAIN YOURSELF WITH IT PRIVATELY. That is an abuse of the gift, and the entire 14th chapter of I Corinthians is written to correct that abuse.

If it is real, don't abuse it by using it for personal edification and enjoyment. Use it as intended...to win unbelievers. However, if the sailors don't hear in their language, you've been deceived. The gift is counterfeit, so drop it!

The Apostle Paul, trained at the feet of Gamaliel, one of the three great rabbinical teachers of all time, was well schooled in the art of speech. Language, oratory, and speech were his stock and trade. He knew when to be tender and when to be strong. He knew when to be gentle and when to be tough. He knew when to be quiet and when to assert himself. He knew when to be demanding and judgmental, and the Corinthian church taxed his every resource as he reached for satire, hyperbole, and every forensic tool at his disposal to attempt to correct a church totally given over to error. What appears on the surface to be support of the gift as used by Charismatics today, may only be properly seen, completely to the contrary, as an attempt to correct the abuse of the gift when every verse of the chapter is interpreted from this perspective: I CORINTHIANS 14 IS SATIRE PURE AND SIMPLE. PAUL IS NOT ENCOURAGING PRIVATE

PRAYING IN TONGUES BY BELIEVERS. HE IS REBUKING IT WITH HOLY SARCASM. As a master of his art, the apostle knew precisely the tools of speech with which to communicate the truth which the church at Corinth so desperately needed.

The use of "holy sarcasm" or "satire" was commonly employed to emphasize truth by Biblical writers as well as our Lord Himself. You may be skeptical of this fact, but the Bible is full of it. Plato said satire was among the most commonly used methods of the ancients—in communicating truth to correct error. Webster says that satire is a literary device in which follies or abuses are exposed by holding them up to ridicule. Far different from humor, satire is only used to instill truth by the discipline of rebuke. In other words, the intent of satire is not simply to be funny, but with a view to correction. And it is as stated, a common Biblical rhetorical device. Let us briefly examine a Biblical example of satire.

> *Then again called they the man that was blind, and said unto him, Give God the praise: we know that this man is a sinner: He answered and said, Whether he be a sinner or no, I know not: one thing I know, that, whereas I was blind, now I see: Then said they to him again, What did he to thee? How opened he thine eyes? He answered them, I have told you already, and ye did not hear: wherefore would ye hear it again? Will ye also be his disciples?*
>
> John 9:24-27

In this simple story the Pharisees discuss with the parents of a boy Jesus had healed, the authority of the Christ who had healed him. Finally, the boy himself responds to the Pharisees with the piercing question, "I have already told you the story and ye did not hear. Why do you want to hear it again? WILL YE ALSO BE HIS DISCIPLES?" *The young man knew full well the Pharisees had no interest in being Jesus' disciples. His question was satirical.*

In studying Paul's reference to the gift of interpretation, it becomes obvious in context that he is attempting to present a comprehensive study of the abuse of the language gift at Corinth. Every conceivable type of situation that might arise must be covered. As far back as the 21st and 22nd verses he rebukes them for not using the gift as a sign to unbelievers as the prophets prophesied. In verse 23 he more specifically states "by using it wrongly, they will cause unbelievers who come into their church fellowship to think they are crazy." The gift is to be used out in the world.

Here he covers with satire a situation that might arise if an unbeliever came out of the world and into the church. Here, too, it must be used properly, not as they were using it, but used to witness to the man who visited their church who could not speak their language. In verse 24 he says, "If you all preach to him—testify to him in his own language, he will be converted and you will all have a part in it." The result stated in verse 25 is that "He will worship your God and testify that your message is true." In verse 26 he is saying, "If this is the proper way the gift is to be used to witness to the lost under the specific condition in which an unsaved person comes into the church, then why is there no order in your service?" Again one may see the device of satire employed. In verse 27 he says in context, "When in the service, someone witnesses to an unsaved visitor in this manner using the gift to testify to him in his own language, even then should it be done by no more than two or at the most three. Of course, that is not even to be done unless there is someone there to interpret." Interpret what? "Interpret what he has said for the sake of the church so that they can hear what is going on and be edified. For the primary purpose of a church service is to edify the Christians." If this is not the case, if no interpreter be present, then the witness cannot be given at all. The desire to witness to the lost visitor in his language must become subordinate to the greater need of the church to be edified by preaching. In such a situation, the person with the gift must not use it. He must sit quietly and pray. Verse 28 does not say, "He must pray in tongues to himself" or "Pray to God in tongues." It just says, "Be quiet and pray to God." Nothing is said or inferred about sitting quietly and talking to God in tongues.

There is nowhere in New Testament canon to suggest that a message in a service was a Heavenly message or a Heavenly revelation or a prophetic utterance to the church either controllable or uncontrollable. It was a simple witness of the Gospel in his own language to a church visitor who could not understand the language of the worshipers. Speaking in languages not learned is a miraculous tool of evangelism and proclamation.

The Mormons have built a doctrine of baptizing for the dead from a passage in I Corinthians 15 that is pure satire. It is of interest to note that following the entire satirical 14th chapter, Paul's method of satire continues into chapter 15 in the abuse of spiritual gifts in chapter 14, paralleled by the abuse of doctrine in chapter 15.

Moreover, brethren, I declare unto you the gospel which I preached unto you, which also ye have received, and wherein ye stand; By which also ye are saved, if ye keep in memory what I preached unto you, unless ye have believed in vain. For I delivered unto you first of all that which I also received, how that Christ died for our sins according to the scriptures; And that he was buried, and that he rose again the third day according to the scriptures.

I Corinthians 15:1-4

Now if Christ be preached that he rose from the dead, how say some among you that there is no resurrection of the dead? But if there be no resurrection of the dead, then is Christ not risen: And if Christ be not risen, then is our preaching vain, and your faith is also vain. Yea, and we are found false witnesses of God; because we have testified of God that he raised up Christ: whom he raised not up, if so be that the dead rise not. For if the dead rise not, then ye are yet in your sins. Then they also which are fallen asleep in Christ are perished. If in this life only we have hope in Christ, we are of all men most miserable.

I Corinthians 15:12-19

For he hath put all things under his feet. But when he saith all things are put under him, it is manifest that he is excepted, which did put all things under him. And when all things shall be subdued unto him, then shall the Son also himself be subject unto him that put all things under him, that God may be all in all. Else what shall they do which are baptized for the dead, if the dead rise not at all? Why are they then baptized for the dead?

I Corinthians 15:27-29

Here Paul appears to be introducing a strange new doctrine, that of being baptized for the dead. The grossest of perversions from Gospel truth have been built upon misinterpretation of the clear intent of this passage. Is Paul teaching that we can procure salvation for other long-since dead and gone by being baptized in their behalf? NOT IN A MILLION YEARS!

Baptizing for the dead WAS being done by the Corinthian church. We are not surprised to find this for there was virtually no truth that they had not perverted. Mingled with this error, they were teaching that resurrection was not a reality. In the opening four verses of the chapter, Paul has introduced the theme of the chapter by making it clear that resurrection not only is a reality, but that Christ's own resurrection stands at the very heart of the Gospel. Following a beautiful defense of the truth of resurrection, Paul inserts a final satirical jab in verse 29 when he says, "If you don't believe in the resurrection of the dead—if you accept no life-after-death, then why do you practice baptizing for those who are already dead to attempt to assure them of eternal after-life in which you yourself do not believe?" Is this to be construed as doctrinal support for procuring the salvation of dead people by baptizing in their behalf from the pen of one whose entire theology is built on a salvation of grace apart from works? ABSOLUTELY NOT! It is satire pure and simple.

Perhaps the two best examples of satire in the New Testament came from none other than our Lord Himself. The first is to be found in Matthew 26:47-50:

And while he yet spake, lo, Judas, one of the twelve, came, and with him a great multitude with swords and staves, from the chief priests and elders of the people. Now he that betrayed him gave them a sign, saying, Whomsoever I shall kiss, that same is he: hold him fast. And forthwith he came to Jesus, and said, Hail, master; and kissed him. And Jesus

said unto him, Friend, wherefore art thou come? Then came
they, and laid hands on Jesus, and took him.

In the fiftieth verse Jesus calls Judas "friend." Does He mean it?
Is He grateful for this tragedy of betrayal? Has it, indeed, proven
Judas to be a warm no faithful friend? Not at all. Jesus is saying, in
essence, "Fine friend you are, Judas." It is satire pure and simple.
Another example of satire used by our Lord is found in John 8:3-
7. Jesus' statement, "You that are without sin cast the first stone,"
was not intended to bring about the stoning of the woman. It was
intended to bring about a sharp rebuke to the pride of the Pharisees.

Let us make a brief examination of part of I Corinthians 14 and
see how easily it may be interpreted in light of our understanding of
the chapter as the use of satire to correct an abuse of a sign gift to
unbelievers.

Verse 1 — *Follow after charity, and desire spiritual gifts, but*
rather that ye may prophesy.

Paul asserts the value of love and the beauty of gifts, but emphasizes the *priority* of preaching. The passion of the heart of the great
evangelist is that the world, both Jew and Gentile, may come to
Christ. The instrumentality of world evangelism is the proclamation or preaching of the Gospel here referred to as "prophecy." Old
Testament prophecy was a foretelling of the future. New Testament
prophecy is the preaching of the Gospel. In verse one, Paul gives a
clear presentation of the motivation for world evangelism—love;
the supporting force to world evangelism—sign gifts to validate
the Gospel; and the priority of the means of world evangelism—
prophecy (preaching).

Verse 2 — *For he that speaketh in an unknown tongue spea-*
keth not unto men, but unto God: for no man understandeth
him; howbeit in the spirit he speaketh mysteries.

Immediately Paul attacks the abuse of the gift. There is no
question that they were exercising the gift in private. They were

addressing God. Paul is rebuking them for speaking to God, rather than speaking unto men as it was intended. Of what use is the gift if no man can understand? It is all a mystery to the hearer. It is of no value to speak to God in an unknown tongue—the purpose was to speak to men. The King James version uses the expression, "He that speaketh in an unknown tongue, speaketh unto God." The literal rendition of the Greek, however, has no definite article before the word "God," and may also be translated, "speaketh unto A God," not specifically unto our one true God. Paul may well be saying, "You are just jabbering to a god. That is what you did when you were unsaved. That was your practice when you made ecstatic utterances to a thousand unknown pagan deities."

Verse 3—*But the that prophesieth speaketh unto men to edification, and exhortation, and comfort.*

The thrust of the Gospel is the thrust of preaching. We are to proclaim the Word of God unto lost men. They are to be exhorted (follow Christ), built up in Christ (edified), and comforted.

Verse 4—*He that speaketh in an unknown tongue edifieth himself; but he that prophesieth edifieth the church.*

You are not using the gift as intended. The gift is to impress the lost and win him to Christ. And what are you doing with it? You are abusing it. You are playing with it. You are using it on yourself. You are only enjoying its use to edify yourself. The gift is to edify the lost by winning them to Christ. But better than that is the gift of preaching (prophecy) to edify the church.

Verse 5—*I would that ye all spake with tongues, but rather that ye prophesied: for greater is he that prophesieth than he that speaketh with tongues, except he interpret, that the church may receive edifying.*

Of course he wished they all spoke with tongues. I, too, wish you all spoke with tongues, and I wish with Paul that tongues were exercised as they were supposed to be. Would to God that every Christian was on the pagan mission field winning the lost. But superior to that is the preaching of the Word to the church to edify and build up strong believers. And why? That our lost generation might be benefited by having thousands of built-up strong Christians go out among the unsaved world exercising the gift of languages as intended to win millions to Christ.

> Verse 6—*Now, brethren, if I come unto you speaking with tongues, what shall I profit you, except I shall speak to you either by revelation, or by knowledge, or by prophesying, or by doctrine?*

Of what profit is it if we all sit around and jabber to ourselves and God while the world goes to hell? My teaching, when I speak to you, is far superior to that. I can only edify you by teaching you some revelation from God or by imparting knowledge to you or by preaching to you or by teaching you sound doctrine.

> Verses 7-11—*And even things without life giving sound, whether pipe or harp, except they give a distinction in the sounds, how shall it be known what is piped or harped? For if the trumpet give an uncertain sound, who shall prepare himself to the battle? So likewise ye, except ye utter by the tongue words easy to be understood, how shall it be known what is spoken? For ye shall speak into the air. There are, it may be, so many kinds of voices in the world, and none of them is without signification. Therefore if I know not the meaning of the voice, I shall be unto him that speaketh a barbarian, and he that speaketh shall be a barbarian unto me."*

Does not even life teach you the inferiority of garbled, indistinct gibberish? Far better to say a word easy to be understood which can help us all. If I do not speak clearly and hear clearly while others speak clearly, we are all going to sound like a bunch of crazy barbarians to each other and to the world. HOW SEVERE THE ABUSE MUST HAVE BEEN.

Verse 12—*Even so ye, forasmuch as ye are zealous of spiritual gifts, seek that ye may excel to the edifying of the church."*

Paul encourages them that they are zealous of spiritual gifts, but exhorts them to keep in perspective the priority of the body-edifying gifts above the sign gifts for unbelievers. And why is this? It is because shepherds do not give birth to sheep—sheep give birth to sheep. The purpose of the church leaders, teachers, and preachers is to give priority to strengthening believers, thereby building a healthy body. Then those mature, edifying believers can, in turn, exercise their sign gifts to an unbelieving world and win many to Christ.

Verses 13-16—*Wherefore let him that speaketh in an unknown tongue pray that he may interpret. For if I pray in an unknown tongue, my spirit prayeth, but my understanding is unfruitful. What is it then? I will pray with the spirit, and I will pray with the understanding also: I will sing with the spirit, and I will sing with the understanding also. Else when thou shalt bless with the spirit, how shall he that occupieth the room of the unlearned say Amen at thy giving of thanks, seeing he understandeth not what thou sayest?*

This passage may be interpreted correctly only in light of beginning with the conclusion (verse 16) toward which it moves and working backward. Paul is still rebuking them for using the gift on themselves rather than the unsaved world. The commission of the church is the proclamation of the Gospel to the lost. Suppose an unlearned, ignorant, lost person comes into your fellowship. If you are not talking sense in a language he can understand, he cannot even say so much as an "amen" to a simple prayer of thanksgiving such as might be said before a meal. You are speaking in unknown tongues in front of each other and God, but you ought to be giving priority to understanding what you are saying because if it is not clearly stated and understood, it is all unfruitful. "It is fine," he says (verse 15), "to pray with a sense of the power of the Spirit and to sing that way also." But, *not without understanding.* You and everyone else must know what is being said. Instead of wanting to show off your gift, you should be wishing to interpret so someone can understand and be benefited. The wrongful, gibberishing use of the gift in a manner no one understands is not only not giving understanding to you or to your fellows, but it will confound an unbeliever who comes in and cannot even get anything out of such an elemental thing as a table grace. THE PURPOSE OF A GIFT IS TO WITNESS TO AN UNSAVED WORLD. The abusive manner in which you are using it is not only failing to accomplish that purpose, it is further accomplishing nothing at all, and even confounds those unsaved people who ought to be being benefited by its proper usage.

Verse 17—*For thou verily givest thanks well, but the other is not edified.*

Oh, yes, you are trying to give thanks to God as well as you know how, but nothing is accomplished by it, no one is helped by it, none are edified because you use it selfishly and wrongly.

Verse 18—*I thank my God, I speak with tongues more than ye all.*

It is likely that at this juncture of the letter, Paul is thinking that many of the Corinthians were saying, "Aha! But what do you know about speaking in tongues, and what right have you to instruct us?" So Paul simply pauses, as he often does, to validate his authority to speak on the subject. "Don't think," he says, "I don't know what I am talking about—I am an authority on the subject—I speak with tongues more than you all." Of course he did. HE WAS A MISSIONARY MORE THAN THEM ALL. HE WAS AN EVANGELIST MORE THAN THEM ALL. HE TRAVELED THE UNSAVED, PAGAN WORLD ON THE FRONTIER CUTTING EDGE OF EVANGELISM AND PRACTICED THE GIFT AS INTENDED MORE THAN ALL THE REST OF THEM WHO WERE ABUSING IT PUT TOGETHER.

Verse 19—*YET IN THE CHURCH I had rather speak five words with my understanding, that by my voice I might teach others also, than ten thousand words in an unknown tongue.*

The first four words of this verse give great support to the argument I have just stated in verse 18. He spoke in tongues more than them all because he traveled as an evangelist more than them all. YET, IN THE CHURCH, he prefers a few words that are understood than thousands in an unknown tongue. THE PLACE FOR KNOWLEDGE, FOR TEACHING, FOR SOUND DOCTRINE TO EDIFY THE BELIEVERS IS IN THE CHURCH. THE PLACE FOR THE GIFT OF LANGUAGES IS NOT IN THE CHURCH. IT IS IN THE UNSAVED WORLD AS AN INSTRUMENT OF EVANGELISM.

Verse 20—*Brethren, be not children in understanding: howbeit in malice be ye children, but in understanding be men.*

Here Paul makes a plea that these childish, selfish, immature Corinthian believers would mature and understand the proper use of the gift.

Verses 21-22—*In the law it is written, With men of other tongues and other lips will I speak unto this people; and yet for all that will they not hear me, saith the Lord. Wherefore tongues are for a sign, not to them that believe, but to them that believe not: but prophesying serveth not for them that believe not, but for them which believe.*

This quote from Isaiah 28:11-12 is the heart of the chapter and the argument which OUGHT to rest the matter once and for all. Isaiah said, "With men of other languages, God would speak unto this people." Unto what people? Israel. The first use of the gift as seen in Acts 2 was, indeed, to Israel, then to the one-half Israelites in Samaria, then to those who would become spiritual Israelites—the Gentiles in Acts 10, and finally to the full Israelites who had only heard half a message (Acts 19). And what is the result of it all—*yet they will not believe*. That is to say, "Not yet," will they believe, for Paul makes it clear that eventually all Israel will be saved when all of these signs have had their cumulative effect and the final sign of the Messiah coming in glory brings about the conversion of them all (Romans 9:10-11).

> Verse 23—*If therefore the whole church be come together into one place, and all speak with tongues, and there come in those that are unlearned, or unbelievers, will they not say that ye are mad?*

Some churches take delight in calling themselves "The Charismatic Center" of their city of state. *What a pity that Charismatics get together like a covey of quail and practice the sign gifts on each other rather than on the cutting edge of missions and evangelism in the world.* Those unbelievers who see you doing so will think you are crazy. Is the gift of languages intended to make unbelievers think Christians are crazy or to think that they have the truth when they urge Christ upon them? Verse 23 again makes it clear Paul is attempting to correct the abuse of the gift in the Corinthian church. *I do not deny the gift of tongues. It is a valid, Biblical and real gift.* I do deny that Charismatics are like the Corinthians, using it as it was intended.

> Verses 24-25—*But if all prophesy, and there come in one that believeth not, or one unlearned, he is convinced of all, he is judged of all: And thus are the secrets of his heart made manifest; and so falling down on his face, he will worship god, and report that God is in you of a truth.*

If, rather than all of you speaking in tongues, all of you preach, that is, all of you are teaching and preaching the truth of the Gospel with clarity, then unbelievers will be convicted, persuaded, and converted, and all of you collectively will have had a part in bringing them under the conviction of God's judgment and subsequently to conversion. And this, not entertaining yourself in your prayer closet, is what tongues/languages is all about.

John McArthur's commentary on I Corinthians adds a great deal of clarity.

> *If I speak with the tongues of men and of angels, but do not have love, I have become a noisy gong or a clanging cymbal.* (13:1)

In verses 1-2 Paul uses considerable hyperbole. To make his point he exaggerates to the limits of imagination. Using various examples, he says, "If somehow I were able to do or to be… to the absolute extreme, but did not have love, I would be absolutely nothing." In the spirit of the love about which he is talking, Paul changes to the first person. He wanted to make it clear that what he said applied as fully to himself as to anyone in Corinth.

First Paul imagines himself able to speak with the greatest possible eloquence, **with the tongues of men and of angels.** Although *glossa* can mean the physical organ of speech, it can also mean language—just as it does when we speak of a person's "mother tongue." **Tongues**, therefore is a legitimate translation, but I believe that *languages* is a more helpful and less confusing rendering.

In the context there is no doubt that Paul here includes the gift of speaking in languages (see 12:10, 28: 14:4-6, 13-14; etc.). That is the gift the Corinthians prized so highly and abused so greatly.

Paul's basic point in 13:1 is to convey the idea of being able o speak all sorts of languages with great fluency and eloquence, far above the greatest linguist or orator. That the apostle is speaking in general and hypothetical terms is clear from the expression **tongues…of angels**. There is no biblical teaching of a unique or special angelic language or dialect. In the countless records of their speaking to men in Scripture, they ALWAYS speak in the language of the person BEING addressed. There is no indication that they have a heavenly language of their own that men could learn. Paul simply is saying that, were he to have the ability to speak with the skill and eloquence of the greatest men, even with angelic eloquence, he would only **become a noisy gong or a clanging cymbal** if he did **not have love**. The greatest truths spoken in the greatest way fall short if they are not spoken in love. Apart from love, even one who speaks the truth with supernatural eloquence becomes so much noise.

I heard recently that 50% of Southern Baptist pastors believe in a PRIVATE PRAYER LANGUAGE. Add that to the latest controversy over "Calvinism," and perhaps we should change our name to "The Southern Bapti-teryan-costal Convention."

Chapter 13

Let's Roll

R egardless of whatever needs we may have, the Southern Baptist
Convention is still God's greatest instrument for missions and
world evangelism in our time. No institution goes forward without
struggle. No ministry advances without faith. As we continue to
probe, explore, self-examine and commit ourselves to the future, let
us never forget the best is still yet to come. Our Lord is coming soon,
and as we approach Armageddon, the ultimate showdown between
good and evil in this world, I'm happy to say that Southern Baptists
and other evangelical groups are emerging strong in the fray and are
faithful to our Lord and His Great Commission.

There's a wonderful story in the book of Numbers that is replete
with truth analogous to who and where we are today. It is the story of
the conquest of the land of Canaan to which God had finally brought
Israel after a mighty struggle in the wilderness. Let's read this story
taken from Numbers 13:17-21, 27-30 and 14:11, 26-32.

> *And Moses sent them to spy out the land of Canaan, and
> said unto them, Get you up this way southward, and go up
> into the mountain:*
> *And see the land, what it is, and the people that dwelleth
> therein, whether they be strong or weak, few or many; And
> what the land is that they dwell in, whether it be good or
> bad; and what cities they be that they dwell in, whether in*

tents, or in strong holds; And what the land is, whether it be fat or lean, whether there be wood therein, or not. And be ye of good courage, and bring of the fruit of the land. Now the time was the time of the firstripe grapes. So they went up, and searched the land from the wilderness of Zin unto Rehob, as men come to Hamath.

Numbers 13:17-21

And they told him, and said, We came unto the land whither thou sentest us, and surely it floweth with milk and honey; and this is the fruit of it. Nevertheless the people be strong that dwell in the land, and the cities are walled, and very great: and moreover we saw the children of Anak there. The Amalekites dwell in the land of the south: and the Hittites, and the Jebusites, and the Amorites, dwell in the mountains: and the Canaanites dwell by the sea, and by the coast of Jordan. And Caleb stilled the people before Moses, and said, Let us go up at once, and possess it; for we are well able to overcome it.

Numbers 13:27-30

And the LORD said unto Moses, How long will this people provoke me? and how long will it be ere they believe me, for all the signs which I have shewed among them?

Numbers 14:11

And the LORD spake unto Moses and unto Aaron, saying, How long shall I bear with this evil congregation, which murmur against me? I have heard the murmurings of the children of Israel, which they murmur against me. Say unto them, As truly as I live, saith the LORD, as ye have spoken in mine ears, so will I do to you: Your carcasses shall fall in this wilderness; and all that were numbered of you, according to your whole number, from 20 years old and upward which have murmured against me. Doubtless ye shall not come into the land, concerning which I swore to make you dwell therein, save Caleb the son of Jephunneh, and Joshua the son of Nun. But your little ones, which ye said should be a prey, them will I bring in, and they shall know the land which ye have despised. But as for you, your carcasses, they shall fall in this wilderness.

Numbers 14:26-32

I see four tremendous truths to encourage our hearts at this wonderful moment of opportunity in world history before the return of our Lord.

1. God is never pleased when His children are content to simply stand still. The Great Commission has not been revoked, and the world still awaits the Gospel. God did not bring the children of Israel to the Jordan to simply stand and look longingly across its shimmering waters into the fruitful land of opportunity. The journey had been long and difficult, and the prize lay just before them. Whatever God wants for your church, it is not to "do nothing." God is not pleased when we are not on the go and on the move for Him.

Everything about the Gospel is onward, upward. Climb the next mountain; ford the next stream; cross the next river; reach the unreachable star. More, more, more! God cannot be pleased if we are satisfied with the status quo. The Dotsun Motor Company, before they became Nissan, had a slogan, "WE ARE DRIVEN." My fellow Southern Baptists, we are driven too. We are a driven people; driven to the ends of the earth by the Great Commission; driven to the end of time by the soon coming of Christ; driven to the ends of our lives and fortunes by our love for Jesus and desire to make Him known to a perishing world.

I have noticed one common denominator in all the great growing churches. There is a Holy restlessness. They are a driven people. They will not be satisfied. They must give the next dollar, win the next soul, start the next program, call the next staff member, build the next building—on, on, on; upward, upward; more, more, more. It's time to rally. It's time to let bygones be bygones, to rejoice in the victories of the past, to glory in an inerrant Gospel for which many have fought and paid so huge a price, time to rejoice in the beachhead that's been established. For the greatest Christian army in history, 16 million Southern Baptists, to do less is not acceptable.

Remember God is never pleased when a church, a ministry, let alone an entire denomination is simply bogged down in yesterday, secondary issues, or uncertainty about tomorrow. It's onward and upward, and it's right now for Southern Baptists. If we are to know His blessing, we must move out in an unprecedented manner to reach the lost, preach the Gospel, plant new churches and send missionaries.

2. There's always a reason not to go forward. Unfortunately, ten of the spies said "we can't do it, there are too many obstacles; there are too many problems." Only two had the faith to trust God and move out. "There were giants in the land," the ten said. "We look like grasshoppers in their sight." "They have armies and fortified cities. We have only sticks and stones and slingshots." If you want to stand still, you can find an excuse to do it. Going forward takes faith; it takes unity; it takes courage and purpose.

In my lifetime, I have lived through World War II, Korea, Vietnam, Kosovo, Iraq, Afghanistan, and uncounted others. I've seen materialism, secularism, humanism, liberalism, Nazism, fascism and the new morality—the same old immorality. We've lived through Chapaquidic, Watergate, Monicagate, and the end is not yet. The stock market's up; the stock market's down. Communism lifts its head again in many places. Terrorism abounds. The Near East is aflame. How easy it would be to pull in our missionaries, stop our programs, silence our pulpits, close our checkbooks and say, "No, no more, there are too many problems."

Need I remind you that throughout the history of the Christian faith, God's people have always gone forward in the most difficult times? In fact, He often paints us into a corner, as He did with Gideon, to show His glory. In the first century the Roman Empire was a hostile place to live. Every thing about the environment said, "Not now, slow down, go into hiding, save yourself." Christians were being tortured, tormented, beheaded, tarred and feathered, burned at the stake and thrown to wild beasts. But the Church had her greatest growth during the days of the Roman Empire.

The same is true of China. When China closed to the Gospel in 1946, it is said that there were three million Christians there. And when Westerners were again allowed into Communist China

30 years later, what did they find? A church persecuted, a church living underground, a church existing against impossible odds? Yes indeed, but a church that has grown to well over 30 million. And that number today is over a 100 million.

In your own church, you will always find an excuse not to pledge, not to build, not to give, not to sacrifice, not to start that new ministry or build that new building. It's always been that way. It will always be that way. We live in hostile territory. This is the devil's world. We live in enemy territory, just passing through for a little while, and it's always going to be tough. But what a mistake we make when we get our eyes on the problem and not on the solution. Southern Baptists must never forget, the world is our parish, and Jesus is our message, and the Great Commission to the ends of the earth still pulsates with every beat of our heart. Onward, upward, more, Southern Baptists, and the time is now.

3. The decision to go forward is always made in faith. God didn't say, "Why don't they understand me?"—"Why can't they analyze Me?"—"Why can't they figure Me out?"—He said, "Why don't they BELIEVE ME?" When they came to the Red Sea, thank God Moses didn't say, "If that water would ever split, I'd get in it." No, he committed in his heart by faith that he was going forward. He raised the rod and said, "Stand still, children of Israel, and watch what God's going to do." The waters never part until the decision to act is made in faith. The light never comes on until you turn the switch. If you wait for the light before you turn the switch, you will remain in darkness.

Throughout 30 years at First Baptist Church Houston, we made many decisions to call new staff, build new buildings, start new programs and conduct many new ministries. Can I tell you that we never had the money to do any of them? We just did them in faith. God blessed us because of our faith. May your church never stand still because of lack of faith. God blesses faith; God honors faith. Those who commit are those who are blessed. Those who go forward trusting the Lord are never disappointed. God has never failed anyone who followed God in faith since Abraham departed from Haran, and He's not going to fail you. He's not going to disappoint your church. He's not going to let us down. God has set before our churches and our convention and open door, which no man can close. Never forget the old spiritual,

> We've come this far by faith, trusting in the Lord.
> Trusting in His Holy Word, He's never failed us yet.
> Oh, oh, oh, we can't turn back; we've come this far by faith.
> Don't be discouraged by the trouble in the world.
> This old Church will still be standing when Satan's fiery
>   darts have all been hurled.
> Oh, we've come this far by faith; we've come this far by
>   faith.

4. The difference in going forward and not going forward is enormous. God was not pleased. He said, "Why can't these people trust me, seeing all I've done for them in the past. Where's their faith? Why can't they believe Me for one more miracle, one more provision?" But they would not, and it cost them dearly. The Lord said, "Only those few of you who did believe Me, and all the people 20 and under, are going into my land to enjoy the heritage I have provided for them. All of you who grumbled, disbelieved, were divisive and small in your faith are going to take another lap around Mount Sinai and keep marching until you die off and your carcasses are consumed in the wilderness." WHAT A CHALLENGE TO US! May your church, your ministry and our beloved Southern Baptist Convention never, but never, but never stop our missionary advance. We must go forward in faith.

I love the book of Revelation. I have been a student of Eschatology for more than 40 years. But I confess, I do not know everything there is to know about the future judgments and coming world. But I do know this, if it should be this way, the saddest day you will ever live will be to see the story of your life or your church or denomination videoed across the screen of Heaven with a detailed account of exactly who you were, what you did and what you had. And then have God show you another video entitled "IT MIGHT HAVE BEEN." What a sad day when we see what we were and realize what we might have been. Holiness, integrity, humility, faith, unity; all these things are essential in a ministry or in a denomination. May we work together to find unity. May we major on the majors. May we never compromise the purity of the Gospel or the lordship and divinity of the Lord Jesus Christ. Without Him, men are lost. He is our only message; He is our only hope.

When Flight 92 went down on 9/11 in the fields of Pennsylvania, Todd Beamer called his wife Lisa from the bathroom and did his best over a cell phone to tell her terrorists had taken over the plane. After they prayed the Lord's Prayer, His last words to here were "Let's roll." Sounds good to me.

LaVergne, TN USA
22 August 2009
155538LV00004B/38/A